WHAT TO STUDY

Studying Organizations:
Innovations in Methodology

PROJECT ON INNOVATIONS IN METHODOLOGY
FOR STUDYING ORGANIZATIONS

Project Planning Committee

Thomas J. Bouchard, *University of Minnesota*
Joel T. Campbell, *Educational Testing Service*
David L. DeVries, *Center for Creative Leadership*
J. Richard Hackman (Chair), *Yale University*
Joseph L. Moses, *American Telephone and Telegraph Company*
Barry M. Staw, *University of California, Berkeley*
Victor H. Vroom, *Yale University*
Karl E. Weick, *Cornell University*

Project Sponsorship and Administration

The volumes in this series (listed above) are among the products of a multi-year project on innovations in methodology for organizational research, sponsored by Division 14 (Industrial and Organizational Psychology) of the American Psychological Association.

Support for the project was provided jointly by the Organizational Effectiveness Research Program of the Office of Naval Research (Bert T. King, Scientific Officer), and by the School Management and Organizational Studies Unit of the National Institute of Education (Fritz Mulhauser, Scientific Officer). The central office of the American Psychological Association contributed its services for the management of project finances.

Technical and administrative support for the project was provided by the Center for Creative Leadership (Greensboro, NC) under the direction of David L. DeVries and Ann M. Morrison.

STUDYING
ORGANIZATIONS:
Innovations
in Methodology
6

WHAT TO STUDY

GENERATING AND DEVELOPING RESEARCH QUESTIONS

by
John P. Campbell, Richard L. Daft,
and **Charles L. Hulin**

Published in cooperation with Division 14 of the
AMERICAN PSYCHOLOGICAL ASSOCIATION

SAGE PUBLICATIONS
Beverly Hills / London / New Delhi

For information address:

SAGE Publications, Inc.
275 South Beverly Drive
Beverly Hills, California 90212

SAGE Publications India Pvt. Ltd.
C-236 Defence Colony
New Delhi 110 024, India

SAGE Publications Ltd
28 Banner Street
London EC1Y 8QE, England

Printed in the United States of America

Library of Congress Cataloging in Publication Data

Campbell, John Paul, 1937-
    What to study.

    (Studying organizations : innovations in
methodology ; v. 6)
    "Published in cooperation with Division 14 of the
American Psychological Association."
    Bibliography: p.
    1. Organizational research. 2. Organizational
behavior——Research. 3. Psychological research.
I. Daft, Richard L. II. Hulin, Charles L., 1936-
III. American Psychological Association. Division of
Industrial-Organizational Psychology. IV. Title.
V. Series: Studying organizations ; v. 6.

HD30.4.C35   1982   00.4'33   82-10720
ISBN 0-8039-1871-2
ISBN 0-8039-1872-0 (pbk.)

THIRD PRINTING, 1984

Contents

Preface

J. Richard Hackman

There has been increasing interest in recent years, both in academia and in society at large, in how—and how well—organizations function. Educational, human service, political, and work organizations all have come under close scrutiny by those who manage them, those who work in them, and those who are served by them.

The questions that have been raised are important ones. How, for example. can organizations become leaner (and, in many cases, smaller) as the birthrate and the rate of economic growth decline? Is there a trade-off between organizational productivity and the quality of life at work? Or can life at work and productivity be simultaneously improved? What changes in organizational practices are required to increase the career mobility of traditionally disadvantaged groups in society? How are we to understand the apparent asynchrony between the goals of educational organizations and the requirements of work organizations? How can public services be provided more responsively and with greater cost effectiveness? What new and nondiscriminatory devices can be developed to test, assess, and place people in schools and in industry? The list goes on, and it is long.

Unfortunately, there is reason for concern about our capability to build a systematic base of knowledge that can be used to deal with questions such as these. Available strategies for studying organizations have emerged more or less independently from a variety of disciplines, ranging from anthropology, sociology, and political science to educational, industrial, and organizational psychology. But none of these disciplines appears to be on the verge of generating the kind of knowledge about organizations that will be required to understand them in their full richness and complexity.

Why not? Part of the problem may have to do with the *restrictiveness* of discipline-based research—that is, the tendency of academic disciplines to support specific and focused research paradigms, and to foster intense but narrow study of particular and well-defined research "topics." Another possibility, however, is that the *methodologies* used in research on organizations have been far too limited and conventional.

In general, the methods used in studying organizations have been imported from one or another of the academic disciplines. And while these methods may be fully appropriate for the particular research problems and paradigms that are dominant in the disciplines from which they come, they also may blind those who use them to potentially significant new findings and insights about how organizations operate.

Because the need for higher quality organizational research is pressing, now may be the time to try to break through the constraints of traditional methodologies and seek new approaches to organizational research. This was the thinking of the Executive Committee of Division 14 (Industrial and Organizational Psychology) of the American Psychological Association when, a few years ago, it initiated a project intended to foster innovations in methodology for organizational research. A planning committee was appointed, and support was obtained from the Office of Naval Research and the National Institute of Education. Eighteen scholars were recruited from a variety of disciplines and formed into six working groups to review the state of organizational research methodologies, and to seek innovative approaches to understanding organizations. A three-day conference was held at the Center for Creative Leadership, at which about sixty organizational researchers (representing a variety of disciplinary orientations, and from applied as well as academic settings) reviewed the findings and proposals of the six working groups. The working groups then revised their materials based on the reactions of conference participants, and the six monographs in this series are the result.

The content of the six monographs is wide ranging, from new quantitative techniques for analyzing data to alternative ways of gathering and using qualitative data about organizations. From "judgment calls" in designing research on organizations, to ways of doing research that encourage the *implementation* of the research findings. From innovative ways of formulating research questions about organizations to new strategies for cumulating research findings across studies.

This monograph focuses specifically on innovative ways to find and define research problems and questions. It reviews and evaluates the kinds of problems presently being addressed in industrial and organizational research, explores how research questions were posed in studies that have proved to be especially significant (and in some that turned out to be not so significant), and provides some practical techniques for improving the way organizational researchers find and frame their research questions.

The aspiration of the numerous people who contributed their time and talent to the innovations project (they are listed facing the title page) is that readers of this monograph—and of its companions in the series—will discover here some ideas about methods that can be used to benefit both the quality and the usefulness of their own research on organizations.

—*J. Richard Hackman*
Series Editor

Introduction

☐ As with the other volumes in this series, the general nature of what we have tried to do is a function of the original charge given to us by the Methods Conference Planning Committee. Our task, if we were foolish enough to accept it, would be to explore innovative ways to generate new research problems and refine old ones, and to consider the characteristics that make a particular research question useful or not useful.

The planning committee might have had one or more reasons for incorporating this set of objectives as one of the six major workshops at the conference. They may have felt that questions asking in applied psychology was in desperate straits and that something "needed to be done." They may have concluded that since the formulation of the research question is an integral part of the research process, it was only rational to examine it systematically. Or, they may simply have thought it would be interesting to persuade some of their more gullible colleagues to make a good faith effort to examine this topic in some detail.

The initial reaction of each of the authors was to recoil in fear and apprehension. It does seem very presumptuous to anoint oneself as qualified to tell someone else how to be creative, or to specify what research should be done, or to outline standards for what makes a research question good or bad. Everyone felt uncomfortable from the start, and we continue to feel that way today. Because of these feelings we are sympathetic to the following letter we received in the course of conducting a survey as part of our workshop preparations.

> The world seems to be divided into two groups—those who want to decide what work should be done by others and those who don't. Mostly, I belong to the second group. I know what I want to do, and I am not immune to wishing that the world were fashioned in my image. But my experience tells me that it simply doesn't work for me or anyone else to try to tell others what research they should do.

> My belief is that in social research the best work (most creative, most sustained, most systematic), with largest theoretical import, gets done because of a fortunate mix between the development needs of an investigator and a situation that permits her or his work to be executed well.

> The American Psychological Association Division of Industrial and Organizational Psychology has always seemed to me to be prone to want to tell people what to study. Some of my favorite people do it frequently. I think the alternative is to promote a norm of greater self-awareness among researchers to acknowledge and accept that most of what we *all* do is heavily determined by our needs — regardless of methodology and no matter how "objective" we purport or aspire to be. For me the trick is how to use this behavioral phenomenon in the service of research. But we need to stop denying the phenomena before we can use it, and then we need to train people to understand themselves, the social systems they live in, and the process of harnessing these forces for creative research.

> If this orientation were developed, there would be little need to identify research questions — at least that's my view. It is also a long way from where the model Division 14 person or leader is as I see it.

> Good luck on your venture, but I think it's the wrong way to revitalize organizational psychology.

This is certainly a legitimate position to take and many will be in sympathy with it. However, it is also legitimate to question whether there are systematic ways to foster the creative process or to redirect research efforts in ways that will increase the usefulness of research in particular areas and minimize blind alleys. Surely generating research problems is more than a completely idiosyncratic process that cannot benefit from a systematic examination. Isn't it?

During the course of preparing this material we discovered that we are not the only field to worry about the form and substance of our research questions. Newell (1973) and Jenkins (1980) in cognitive psychology, Meehl (1978) in clinical psychology, and McGuire (1973) in social psychology have all raised questions about the quality and form of the research questions that characterize their respective fields. Some of the collective worries are that (a) too often it is the investigator's favorite method that determines the problem rather than vice versa, (b) the applied *or* theoretical import of much current research is difficult to discover, (c) research questions are faddish to the extreme, (d) many findings are highly specific to specific instrumentation, and (e) the "probability of publication" exerts an undue influence on the choice of problems.

Since many other people in other areas of behavioral science have worried about these same things, it gave us a certain amount of courage to continue. Perhaps some benefit would accrue from a closer examination of the research questions we ask, how we ask them, and how we might make our question asking more useful.

Given the above, it is still the case that we have no more right to pontificate about these issues than any other set of three people in this field. Consequently, our overall strategy was to collect as much relevant data as we could with our limited resources and to provide as much of an empirical base as possible for the inferences and generalizations it seemed useful to make.

SOME ASSUMPTIONS

The overall project incorporated certain basic assumptions, which were as follows.

— Applied psychological research on behavior in organizations is extremely difficult to do. It deals with very important and complex phenomena that are difficult to define and control. It will never be simple, easy, or free of error. We must be careful with the kinds of research "ideals" we create and the kinds of research questions we think it is possible to answer. That is, we should not set impossible goals.

— There surely is no general set of rules for finding and developing research problems that will guarantee successful projects and successful careers. Rather, we will strive to articulate a variety of strategies that enhance the probability of developing interesting and useful research questions and reduce the probability of being nonproductive.

— Over some reasonable time span, useful research questions are characterized not only by their form (e.g., derived from a theory versus not derived from a theory). They are also characterized by their substantive content (e.g., we *do* need studies of racial discrimination in job performance criterion measurement)and by the assumptions they incorporate (e.g., the management value system is appropriate — or inappropriate). Some substantive areas *are* more important than others and we should not shy away from making such judgments or from examining the value system on which such judgments are based.

— Although it is only a part of the total domain of applied psychology, most of the material on which the volume is based comes from the fields as industrial/organizational psychology and organizational behavior. The primary reason is that this is what the authors know best. However, we believe that most of the generalizations we will try to make are not encapsulated within these fields and that they have applicability across a wide spectrum of applied psychology.

GENERAL OBJECTIVES

As translated from the original assignment, our general objectives became the following:

(1) to describe the research questions that are *currently* being asked in our field and to comment upon some of their more interesting characteristics;

(2) to report what various people think are the most important research *needs* that we have and to contrast the questions that *have* been studied with the questions that people think *should* be asked;

(3) to describe the characteristics that seem to distinguish successful question asking from unsuccessful question asking, as it is practiced by some of our more successful researchers;

(4) to illustrate and summarize the principal strategies that might profitably be used to reformulate research questions; and

(5) to illustrate and summarize some of the strategies to be *avoided* when formulating research questions.

THE GENERAL PROCEDURE

To accomplish the above objectives we used a number of strategies varying from sitting in the armchair to collecting data. The basic steps we took included:

(1) surveying the available literature on creativity, research innovation, research shortcomings, historical comments on our field, speculations about the future, and so forth;

(2) content analyzing a sample of the organizational behavioral science research literature to determine the questions that are currently being asked and the form in which they are asked;

(3) surveying a large sample of members of the American Psychological Association's Division of Industrial and Organizational Psychology about what research needs should have high priority in the future;

(4) surveying a small sample of managers and professionals who have the responsibility for defining human resource problems in large organizations;

(5) interviewing, at some length, a sample of established researchers (The respondents were asked to describe a study they had done that they were proud of and a study that they were not so proud of, and might like to forget. For each of these two situations the origins of the research questions, and the way they were developed, were contrasted. We have called this the "within-investigator" study.);

(6) developing a list of "research milestones" in industrial and organizational psychology and conducting a telephone survey of their principal investigators? (the respondents were asked to describe how the idea(s) originated and how the project developed); and

(7) labeling ourselves as experts and indulging in a lot of introspection.

As their primary assignment, Hulin was responsible for the content analysis of the published literature, Campbell carried out the surveys of research needs and research milestones, and Daft was the principal investigator for the "within-persons" interview study of established investigators. Although each author took the lead for one of the major phases of the projects and each wrote a section of the original draft, the final product is a collective effort. We collaborated closely and argued a lot in the planning stages and when preparing the material for presentation as a workshop. Most of the generalizations, inferences, and prescriptions found in the individual chapters are the result of our collective arguments about the state of the field and the meaning of the information we collected. Thus while there was a division of labor, there was not a compartmentalization of ideas, arguments, or conclusions.

INSTRUCTIONAL OBJECTIVES FOR READERS

Since the initial workshop and this monograph are meant to be teaching devices, it was necessary and appropriate to have a set of instructional objectives in mind before proceeding. The general instructional objectives for this particular volume are listed below. That is, it is our intent that readers come away with the following:

(1) some specific knowledges about what the field *is* investigating versus what people think it *should be* investigating;

(2) some specific knowledge about how the more accomplished investigators in our field seem to develop their research questions and what, *if anything*, distinguishes a successful question generation process from an unsuccessful one for these people;

(3) a list of substantive research ideas, at least some of which you might consider seriously in the future;

(4) familiarity with a number of different strategies that can be used to reformulate research questions or otherwise look at a problem differently;

(5) knowledge of some major sins that should be avoided when formulating research questions; and

(6) enough new resource material to make some significant change in the way you teach, or otherwise try to influence, others to generate and develop research problems.

OVERVIEW

The remainder of this volume consists of chapters derived from each major section of the original workshop. Chapter 1 seeks to draw some generalizations about the current state of our research questions by content analyzing a sample of the published literature. Chapter 2 reports the results of a survey of people in the field who were simply asked to suggest the most important research questions that we *should* be asking. Chapter 3 is an attempt to contrast the views of people in organizations with the views of the people in the Division of I/O Psychology reported in Chapter 2. The data here are a bit meager, but some interesting things seemed worth saying. Chapter 4 reports the results of the interview study of established researchers as to how their most and least favorite research projects came to be. Chapter 5 is a brief summary of what happened when one of the authors decided one day to make a list of research milestones in the recent history of industrial and organizational psychology and then called the principal investigators on the telephone and asked them how the research question originated and developed. Controlled research it was not, but the responses were nonetheless interesting, and they complemented the results portrayed in Chapter 4. Chapter 5 is our collective attempt to summarize some available strategies for maximizing the chances of finding interesting research questions and avoiding counterproductive question asking.

We say again that we are uncomfortable about this entire endeavor. Nothing much qualifies us for it that does not qualify hundreds of others.

It seems appropriate at this point to recall an incident from the classroom experience of one of the authors. On one particular day, in the course of talking about motivation issues in general and equity in particular, he complained about the salary differentials for academics versus nonacademics. One uppity member of the class then asked why he stayed in the ivory tower and worked for such low wages. The necessity of thinking of an answer, any answer, was removed by a pragmatist in the back row, who raised his hand and said, "Well, somebody has to do it." We proceed.

1

Questions, Nonquestions, and Unasked Questions from Ten Journal-Years

For an idea to be fashionable is ominous since it must afterwards be always old-fashioned.

— G. Santayana

BACKGROUND

One can identify two informal epistemologies in social science. One describes the process of knowledge accumulation as if a large number of researchers were throwing mud at a wall. The mud that sticks to the wall is knowledge and should be retained. That which falls off is indeed mud and should be discarded. This theory of knowledge accumulation suggests that the more individuals there are throwing different kinds of mud, the more likely it is that some of them will throw something that sticks.

Authors' Note: Many of the individuals who participated in the preparation and collection of data for this chapter were volunteers who donated their time and effort. The freely contributed energies of Mary Roznowski, Cathy Gray, and Stephanie Edwards deserve a special mention. Without their assistance, the lack of heterogeneity in the sample of journals would have been even more cause for concern.

A contrasting approach suggests that knowledge accumulates by means of individuals carefully mapping out areas likely to yield information: prospecting through scree, rubble, and dirt to find the ore-bearing rock. The mapping that precedes the prospecting and mining is based on carefully accumulated knowledge, theory, models specifying what is important, and occasionally, intuition. Careful mapping and pretesting are more likely to lead to the discovery of nuggets of knowledge than random digging; the more carefully the pretesting and mapping, the more likely the discovery of true, rather than false, gold.

These two informal theories of knowledge have much different implications for organizational research. The first suggests that for the field as a whole—the more, the better. More independent investigators from different backgrounds using different techniques to answer different questions will yield more knowledge with greater probabilities of significant advancements. The second says that investigators should be encouraged on the basis of their skills in mapping unexplored areas and extrapolating from the known to the unknown. Parametric studies, based on the careful applications of proven techniques and paradigms, should be encouraged in areas that have been productive in the past.

In spite of the different implications they may have for the field as a whole, they have much the same implications for individual investigators. Both depend heavily on the insights of the individuals asking questions. In the mud-throwing analogy, the probability of finding a substance that adheres to the wall and provides unique information depends in part on individuals avoiding duplicating the efforts of others. "Throw material found in new areas" would be the advice based on this analogy. In the second analogy, careful mapping and exploration should lead to the accumulation of knowledge; advances are made when individual investigators carefully extend research into new areas by asking insightful questions based on past research, explorations, proven techniques, and intuition. Careful phrasing of questions that do not repeat old mistakes, do not follow slavishly through the tailings of others, and build creatively on past findings is an important element in the potential worth of explorations by individuals.

The work by the planning committee on this series of workshops, the acceptance of the workshop assignments by the presenters, the presence of fifty individuals as participants, and the funding by the Office of Naval Research and the National Institute of Education all stand as testimony that a significant number of investigators in applied psychology are disturbed by the kinds of research they see in this area.

Our workshop was asked to prepare and present materials that could be used by investigators to find and ask innovative research questions — how to keep the wolf of triviality away from their research room doors. Innovative is used in this context to identify questions that not only have not been asked before, but whose asking will open new research problems, might resolve long-standing controversies, could provide an integration of different approaches, and might even turn conventional wisdom and assumptions upside down challenging old beliefs.

As a start, we decided to find out what current practice was — what was occupying the time of researchers who were studying individuals behavior in organizations? What questions were being asked and studied in our major empirical and theoretical journals? Based on a knowledge of the current questions that are receiving attention, we could (perhaps) infer the assumptions that were made, the conventional wisdoms that were used, and the research leads that were being followed possibly beyond the point at which attention was repaid with unique information. From this assessment of current interests and questions, one can also make some educated guesses about questions that are not being asked — but perhaps should be. It is when we venture into this latter area and begin discussing questions that should be, but are not, asked that we cease being reporters and chroniclers and become advocates and perhaps even meddlers.

Five relevant journals were selected for reviewing and content coding of the articles and the questions that the articles asked about the behaviors of individuals in organizations. Articles that were straightforward, statistical/methodological expositions or whose content was remote from the topic of this conference were not abstracted. Each of these five journals was surveyed for two years, 1977 and 1979, producing ten journal-years of articles. The ten journal-years of articles and questions were from the *Journal of Applied Psychology, Personnel Psychology, Organizational Behavior and Human Performance, Administrative Science Quarterly,* and *Academy of Management Journal* for the years indicated.

A larger and more heterogeneous sample of journals sampled across more years would have perhaps provided better estimates with smaller sampling variances of the concerns of researchers in this area. However, many of the individuals who participated in this phase of the workshop preparation were volunteers who donated their time and effort.

Every article published in these years and journals on the topic of individuals behavior in organizations was read and abstracted. The major questions asked in the article were extracted. The source of the questions was noted where it could be determined. The questions were then coded into a hierarchical content coding scheme. The major content categories were noted, and under each major category, specific prototypical questions were listed. Each article was placed both in a major question content category on the basis of the questions being asked in the article and into a specific question category subsumed under that major content ara.

Our purposes in developing this content coding of articles and questions was to summarize and communicate the major content interests of researchers without degrading the meanings of the different content categories more than was necessary. We also wanted our prototypical questions within each of the content categories to reflect the richness and variety of research problems in the different areas. The questions should also be able to convey the concerns of specific individual investigators. Clearly some loss of information occurs in the coding. Not all investigators phrase questions similarly, even questions that are operationalized identically. The necessary "leveling" that occurred was unavoidable and, we hope, minimal.

Articles dealing exclusively with very narrow aspects of human factors psychology, such as the legibility of traffic signs, or with knobs-and-dials aspects of engineering psychology were not analyzed beyond the initial categorizations. Although an important area of organizational research, this area has become a coherent subdiscipline of psychology. An enlightened treatment of the research questions being asked in engineering psychology is beyond the scope of this monograph.

It will also become evident during the remainder of this chapter that we attach as much significance to questions that are not asked as to those frequently asked. Determining what is being asked is straightforward; determining what is missing is not. One has further difficulty creating categories into which to place the nonasked questions unless there is a well-articulated meta-theory of what questions should have been asked.

The potential information contained in the nonoccurrence of an event that is free to occur is as great as the information contained in the occurrence of an event that is free not to occur. Examining and categorizing nonoccurrences — in this case, questions that were not asked — is infinitely more difficult because one is not only not sure what should have happened and did not, one is not sure when a nonoccurrence should have occurred. Our attention is necessarily drawn to an event that occurs. We notice it, trivial and repetitious though it may be. Many questions were asked and studied during these ten journal years. These we noticed and categorized. Even more questions were not asked during this time period. Indeed, many should not have been asked. Unfortunately, many also were not asked that probably should have been, but we do not have the palpable evidence of the questions and articles that were stimulated by the asking of the original question from which to infer the innovativeness and importance of the event.

Sir Arthur Conan Doyle once wrote a mystery (*The Hound of the Baskervilles*) in which the most important clue leading to the solution of the crime was the nonoccurrence of an event — a dog did not bark that should have. Of course, it required the deductive powers of Holmes to notice the nonoccurrence and its importance. Most of us are less likely than Holmes to notice nonoccurrences and be able to deduce their importance.

As an exercise, however, it is instructive to both note the contents of the journals in this area and to ask, in a systematic fashion, why questions were not asked about different dependent variables, different populations of respondents, different independent variables, and even different theoretical approaches to the study of behavior in complex organizations. Categorizing the nonasked questions may suggest holes in our knowledge that could be filled in with the answers to but a few innovative questions.

CAVEAT EMPTOR

Several warnings are in order. No necessary relationship should be assumed between the importance of an area (in the cosmic scheme of things) and its popularity as judged by the frequency of occurrence of questions that are studied. Some trivial areas seem to be popular because it is easy to ask questions and data are easy to obtain. Some gaps may exist in our knowledge and may remain relatively unstudied because some areas are very difficult to study. At the same time, some very popular areas are demonstrably important because of the painstakingly developed networks that relate the major concepts of the area to many important behaviors. Whether we are reaching the point of diminishing returns on some much-researched questions is a matter for the reader to judge. As an example from a related area, consider the thousands of studies that have been done on the construct of intelligence. Its antecedents, covariates, consequences, structure, measurement, and practical utility have been studied exhaustively. Perhaps because of this effort, many clinicians, cognitive psychologists, psychometricians, and personnel psychologists will testify that the single most important datum one can have about an individual is his or her score on a standardized general intelligence test.

There may be constructs in organizational research that have been exhaustively studied to the point of diminishing returns. There may be others that are beginning to offer important insights *because* of the many studies done on them. The popularity of an area, to repeat, does not necessarily any positive or negative relation to its importance. The innovativeness of the questions being asked, however, within any given area, may be significantly related to the unique knowledge we have acquired.

Finally, five undergraduate and graduate assistants worked on this project at different times during the eighteen months between the beginning of the research and the preparation of this report. There are very likely errors of count, content coding, abstracting the major questions asked, and even interpretations. These can be attributed to the writer's problems coordinating and supervising this work. There very likely will be readers who know of an article from one of the five journals surveyed during these two years that contradicts one of our statements. Our feeling is that such errors are likely to be minor and will not reverse any of the major points of this chapter.

GENERAL RESEARCH QUESTIONS

Table 1.1 presents the major categorization of the 464 articles read and abstracted from the ten journal-years surveyed. By itself, Table 1.1 is instructive in documenting the content areas of our concern. These results attest to the preoccupations of researchers who publish in the five selected journals with three traditional research areas. Personnel selection and placement

TABLE 1.1 Categories of Empirical and Theoretical Articles from Ten
Journal-Years

Content Category	Subtotals Frequency	Percentage of Total	Frequency	Percentage of Total
Questions about traditional selection and placement			92	20
Performance and criterion measurement	30	06		
Predictor measurement	21	05		
Criterion-centered validity	16	03		
Substantive questions about fairness and discrimination	13	03		
Job analysis	7	02		
Content and construct validity	5	01		
Questions about job satisfaction, job attitudes, and values			72	16
How job satisfaction should be measured	3	01		
How job satisfaction relates to other variables	36	08		
The importance and extent of job satisfaction	3	01		
Attitudes and values and how they relate to behaviors	11	02		
Interrelations among organizational climate, job commitment, and job involvement	15		03	
Role conflict, role ambiguity, and job stress	14	03		
Questions about leadership			42	09
Assessment of leader behavior and performance	19	04		
Determinants of leader behavior and performance	8	02		
Leadership theory	15	03		
Questions about training methods			7	03
How to design training methods	2	—		
How well specific training methods work	3	01		
How training should be evaluated	2	—		

TABLE 1.1 Continued

Content Category	Subtotals			
	Frequency	Percentage of Total	Frequency	Percentage of Total
Additional categories				
Organizational characteristics	35	08		
Motivation theory	20	04		
Individual decision making	17	04		
Turnover and absenteeism	14	03		
Goal setting	13	03		
Group problem solving and decision making	13	03		
Intraorganizational communication	10	02		
Career progression	9	02		
Job design	9	02		
Cross-cultural or cross-national phenomena	8	02		
Performance in unusual environments	8	02		
Ability/interest/personality measurement	7	03		
Operant techniques	6	01		
Collective bargaining and union membership	6	01		
Alternative work schedules	5	01		
Safety and accidents	5	01		
The effects of feedback	4	01		
Statistics and experimental design	4	01		
Data collection methods	4	01		
Relational networks within organizations	3	01		
Equipment and systems	3	01		
Multivariate prediction	3	01		
Organizational strategies	2	—		
Effects of employee ownership	1	—		
Other questions	42	09		
TOTAL	464			

and closely related areas, job satisfaction, and leadership accounted for 45 percent of the articles read from these ten journal-years. The reasons for the popularity of these three areas are probably obvious. Equal Employment Opportunity Commission (EEOC) concerns, Title VII of the 1964 Civil Rights Act, and such court cases as *Griggs* v. *Duke Power* have stimulated a reawakening of research interest in selection, placement, and measurement of job performance.

Research on job satisfaction continues to be frequent probably because an individual's score on a well-designed, standardized job satisfaction scale is related to a number of demonstrably important behaviors — turnover, absenteeism (to a lesser extent), direction of voting in National Labor Relations Board (NLRB) union representation elections, attendance at work when conditions make it difficult, and (more problematic) job stress. Given this range of consequences or correlates of job satisfaction, it is important that sound measures and comprehensive, integrative models of job satisfaction be developed.

Leadership continues to be a content area with a great deal of research activity probably because of the intuitive appeal, the folk wisdom, and the convictions of many practicioners (particularly in the military services) that it is an important variable in organizational functioning. Periodic new developments and conceptualizations of the leadership process continue to appear adding to the long-standing interest and research activity in this area.

We note with some apprehension the relative lack of questions about training. The pervasiveness of legal problems created by the adverse impact of most selection programs on minorities and females could easily stimulate organizations to adopt either minimal hiring standards or even random selection procedures. Success during the training programs that must be established in place of rigorous selection could be used to place individuals into jobs or professions. If training is inexpensive, using a training system as a substitute selection system could be cost effective. However, the legal requirements regarding bias, adverse impact, job relatedness, and overall fairness of the procedures that are imposed on selection systems today will likely be applied by the courts to training programs tomorrow if they are used for that purpose. Because of the past widespread assumptions, in the absence of evidence, about the validity of selection devices, we have been in a race to catch up with the courts decisions and EEOC requirements since *Griggs*. Were training to be substituted for selection, it would be painful indeed to have to go through the same process once again.

There are other areas of inquiry in which but few questions were encountered. Our arbitrary selection of two years accumulation of five journals from among the many candidates probably accounts for a portion of the content distributions. Even with this as a possible explanation, some low frequency categories deserve comment. There is little comfort, for example, in Table 1.1 for those who think there should be more research on unions, unionization, strikes, and the quasi-judicial American industrial relations system. During this period, this area was indeed underresearched.

Cross-cultural research on organizations is being done by organizational researchers but at a rate that belies the projected importance of multinational companies. Performance in unusual environments is studied at a modest rate, albeit at a rate that may reflect the base rate of unusual environments. However, it is somewhat discouraging to note that the unusual environments that are studied are those of interest to human factors specialists — hyperbaric chambers, high-altitude simulations, extremes of heat and cold — and not those that might be created by what some see as future developments and trends in organizational structures. We shall return to this theme frequently in our discussions of the specific research questions that were encountered.

Questions about the effects of different organizational characteristics on relevant responses of organizational members were asked frequently. However, most of the organizational characteristics studied were those that a naive observer might be able to observe and categorize without reference to a theory — size, shape, service versus manufacturing, profit versus nonprofit. There were few studies of the effects of variables that might be generated by new conceptualizations or theories of the purpose of organizations. Research generated by conceptualizing organizations as information-processing systems, sociotechnical systems, or as perceived clusters of roles is not being reported in these journals.

Most distressing of all, at least to those who contributed to this chapter, is the absense of questions about what people, not just managers, *do* in organizations. That is, careful observational work that is necessary to develop taxonomic tables of behavioral patterns is regretably lacking. Few investigators report the results of observational studies whose purpose is to develop the basis of a science of behavior in organizations to replace our emerging science of consistencies among verbal reports obtained on questionnaires. Dimensional and factorial studies of relations among objective behaviors of individuals in organizations are clearly required but few efforts in those directions are to be found in the literature in this area. It has been noted in a different context that "you can observe a lot out there just by looking." We should be doing more looking and categorizing.

We have not documented the nonrandom distributions of questions and content areas listed in Table 1.1 across the different journals surveyed. The unequal distributions are to be expected; few would be surprised at the trends of macro- and microresearch emphases, studies of decision making and human judgments, and relative emphasis on theory that are found in the different journals. Taken as a whole, such trends across journals are unimportant for our overall field of study unless individuals also restrict their reading to those same journals in which they publish.

We also note that the variety of content areas and research questions suggested by Table 1.1 can also be interpreted as a sign of vitality and health of this research area. In spite of the greater concentration of studies in some areas than many might like to see, the apparent wide distribution of research efforts across these areas is encouraging. Although most of the questions have a definite applied flavor to them, there is little evidence that researchers are taking their research questions from what management says is important or are spending time trying to develop lay concepts such as "burn out" or "midcareer crises" into research programs.

SPECIFIC RESEARCH QUESTIONS

JOB ATTITUDES AND JOB PERCEPTIONS (N = 36)

Three prototypical questions that were asked about relations of job satisfaction and other job attitudes with other variables of interest are listed below:

(1) How is job satisfaction related to perceptions of other job and organizational characteristics? (N = 9)

(2) What individual differences/demographic variables correlate with job satisfaction? (N = 8)

(3) What "moderates" the correlation between job satisfaction and performance/turnover/behavior? (N = 5)

The first question, in this and in disguised, mutant forms, is frequently encountered. Unless one were interested in contributing to a developing science of questionnaire behavior, relating verbally reported affect to verbally reported perceptions seems unlikely to produce a significant advance in our knowledge about job attitudes. This does not deny the usefulness of similar questions during early stages of research on many constructs. Our questioning of the value of these studies reflects our assumptions about the state of knowledge today about job attitudes.

The second question is an actuarial question that tells us little about the basic psychology underlying the observations.

Once again, we do not deny the importance of careful developments of networks of relations between important theoretical constructs and objective variables that are important components of a theory or model of job effect. Such questions must indeed be answered. They are necessary and useful steps in the development of any research area. In the case of job satisfaction, that stage of research development seems long past. We need to know what important psychological variables are being summarized by the individual difference/demographic variables that are underlying the observed relations.

The third question produces vivid images of an inwardly self-absorbing, circular triad of studies: Do needs moderate the relation between job satisfaction and performance? Do job satisfaction moderate the relations between needs and performance? Does performance moderate the relations between needs and satisfactions? If all of these combinations of predictors, criteria, and moderators appear in our laundry list of studies to be done, something is seriously wrong with the ways we generate ideas. The theoretical or practical meaningfulness of any set of three-way, moderated relations with every variable serving as predictor, criterion, and moderator in turn is problematic.

OTHER JOB ATTITUDES (N = 13)

A frequently asked question within the general research area of role conflict, role ambiguity, and job stress is:

(1) Do individual or organizational characteristics explain more variance? (N = 4)

A close examination of this question suggests it is a non-question cloaked in a clever disguise. Both individual differences and organizational characteristics can explain variance in an individual dependent variable or in a multivariate set of dependent variables, depending on the variance of each set of characteristics used as predictors and on the content of the dependent variables. If an investigator, either intentionally or inadvertently, samples variables from a very homogeneous set of individual differences, each of which individually has very little variance, it is unlikely that these predictors will account for a great deal of variance in relevant, dependent variables. Organizational characteristics will probably account for more of the variance in the dependent variables that are being studied. Further, with individual variables and organizational characteristics expressed in different metrics, we will never know in which way, or indeed even if, we have stacked the deck.

Attempts to alleviate problems caused by nonequivalent metrics and noncomparable variances by sampling broadly or randomly from the populations of individual variables and organizational characteristics are unlikely to succeed. Random samples and claims of ecological validity require the existence and definition of populations from which samples are drawn and to which generalizations are permissible. Although our knowledge of individuals and individual differences may permit specifications of relevant populations of individuals, our knowledge of inter- or intraorganizational characteristics is not sufficiently developed to permit such claims. Random samples, ecological validity, or equivalent variances from the different sets of independent variables that would allow us to ask this question in a meaningful manner cannot be claimed at this time.

Investigators choices of dependent variables will also predetermine the answers to many investigations of such questions. Individuals drink more beer in bars than in churches. More people take baths in bathrooms than in supermarkets. Contributions of individual differences to variance in beer consumption or bathing can be trivial compared with variance due to situational characteristics. Generalizability of answers to such nonquestions is very limited, suggesting answers to nonquestions are not very informative or generalizable.

Sound theories of individual differences, environmental or organizational characteristics, and structures and meanings of individuals responses are lacking but are required to permit significant increments of knowledge gained from the information provided by answers to such apparently "parametric" and comparative questions. It is true that few industrial and organizational (I/O) researchers are interested in beer drinking or bathing as dependent variables for scientific investigations. It is also true that few would deliberately select dependent variables as extreme as these examples whose variance was to be partitioned. However, without good guidance for our choices of both independent and dependent variables, such comparative nonquestions are best left unasked.

PREDICTOR MEASUREMENT (N = 21)

The following are two prototypical questions about predictor measurements as well as three questions that perhaps should have been asked but were not.

(1) What interview characteristics have the greatest effects on final decisions? (N = 8)

(2) How do different components of assessment centers compare with alternative measures? (N = 3)

(3) No questions about fundamental validity of Thurstonian trait theoretic assumptions.

(4) No questions about item bias.

(5) No questions about adverse impact of predictors with and without measurement bias.

The importance of both questions that were asked is evident. Interviews are probably the most frequently used selection device, either alone or in combination with others, in use today. It is important that we know about both the overall validity of the decisions made on the basis of interviews and about the interviewing process itself as an information-gathering procedure. Assessment centers, referred to in the second question, are both expensive and frequently used for managerial selection. Their utility, as a consequence of their costs and potential benefits, must be investigated.

The importance of the three nonasked questions is more arguable. However, the typical selection study represents a paradigm in which aptitudes, abilities, interests, or other individual characteristics are assessed at one time and are used to predict performance at some later time. The use of this paradigm requires us to assume that assessments of predictor variables obtained in the intial time period remain high-fidelity representations of individuals characteristics at the time when the performance measures are obtained. If indeed performance is a function of individual abilities and aptitudes, a crucial assumption of such prediction studies, the abilities on which performance depends must be those that exist at the time of performance. Only if we assume the validity of a static, trait-theoretic approach to abilities should an assumption of long-term stability of individual differences be made.

Assumptions that are crucial to dominant paradigms in a research area should be questioned and studied. In this case, it appears that the study of the assumptions might yield significant advances in knowledge. Information from two related areas seems to raise questions about the validity of the assumption. Studies of the stability of psychomotor and cognitive performance across time as well as studies of transfer of training both suggest that changes in characteristics of individuals as a function of practice on a criterion task are more to be expected than long-term stability. The variations of both the questions that could be asked and their practical implications for our standard paradigms and legal issues about selection are nearly endless. Perhaps because the Thurstonian trait-theoretic model is so much a dominant part of our *Zeitgeist*, we rarely raise questions about its assumptions.

We similarly encountered no questions about item bias, as opposed to test bias, or about the relative adverse impact of different predictors with different amounts of measurement bias. Our lack of attention to the first of these nonasked questions may be an example of our field reacting to inputs from nonscientific judicial systems rather than from proactively defining the relevant information on which legal decisions should be based. The courts have been concerned almost exclusively with the issues of test fairness or with equity of tests and the decisions made on the basis of such tests. As applied psychologists, we may be able to make our most meaningful contributions to measurement problems or bias at the point of measurement rather than at the point of application. It is in these areas, where we can make significant contributions, that we should be asking our questions.

A related question would be about the relative adverse impact of different predictors. Questions about adverse impact seem frequently to have been asked in an either/or, all or none, fashion. "Does predictor X have an adverse impact against protected minorities?" Alternative questions might be, "Is adverse impact reduced by purging biased items from selection tests? Does removing variance due to measurement bias reduce the adverse impact of our standard selection measures?" Once again, the practical implications of such questions for the entire selection research area are significant and have long-term implications for both legal and basic psychometric issues. It is important to stress that these are questions whose starting point is psychometric theory and not legal assumptions and definitions of test bias or adverse impact.

PERFORMANCE ASSESSMENT (N = 28)

The following are two frequently asked questions (as well as six unasked ones) in the content area of performance assessment/evaluation and criterion measurement.

(1) What rating format is best? (N = 9)

(2) What is best method to reduce halo? (N = 6)

(3) No questions asking if "halo" has any substantive meaning.

(4) No questions asking what underlying or latent trait is being estimated by ratings.

(5) No questions investigating the simultaneous assessment of rater and ratee traits.

(6) No questions about change/stability of performance.

(7) No questions about differentiating between psychometric unreliability and true change.

(8) No questions about scales of performance measurement that directly reflect utility.

The first question seems to assume that one rating form is best or that if there is a best rating format, it can be determined on the basis of one study. The answer, if one even exists, is probably that different rating formats are better for different populations and even for different purposes within the same populations. One study is unlikely to provide such comprehensive evidence or even produce any evidence that can be integrated into a more comprehensive statement. More fundamentally, the question assumes that there exists some rating form and format that is good for some purpose in some population. If we are asking questions about the comparative value of procedures with true but unknown validities of .05 versus .10, we will find answers to our questions. If we rarely ask about the absolute value of the generic procedure — ratings — we will remain uninformed about our ignorance.

The second question makes an equally fundamental assumption: that we want to reduce halo. Perhaps what has been labeled "halo" contains the signal rather than the noise in rating measures. It is possible that differentiating individuals along one overall good/bad dimension is all we can expect from most raters. If this general, overall halo dimension closely parallels the "G" dimension in human abilities, it might suggest that raters are functioning as the *data* about human performance and human abilities — rather than as our multifactor models and theories suggest they should. Questions about the substantive meanings of "halo" should be asked. The lack of substantive meaning should not be assumed.

The second and third unasked questions, taken together, raise a number of interesting problems. Whatever raters are asked to make judgments about individuals' performance levels, there is the possibility that the instrument is providing information about the raters' as well as the ratees' relevant traits. Indeed, in slightly different circumstances and using slightly altered formats, such paradigms have been frequently used to scale judges rather than stimuli. Can simultaneous extraction of rater and ratee traits provide as much information about raters as it does about ratees? Can we use this new information from ratings to improve our knowledge about individuals' performance in organizations?

The next two unasked questions reflect a concern we have for the long-term implications of any study about individuals that takes place in a very constrained time period. Once again, the implicitly assumed theoretical model from which most questions in this area are derived assumes stability rather than change. As a consequence, if we assume that stability is the true nature of things, we treat change, unless we have created it experimentally, as unreliability and error. We seldom, if ever, study naturally occurring change. We must challenge more of our fixed creeds and certitudes about our research areas.

A final not-asked question is concerned with the system of metrics we use to measure job performance. Cronbach and Gleser (1965) presented their utility model of personnel decision making in 1959. This linear interpretation requires that performance be assessed along a utility scale of measurement or that we at least estimate the standard deviations of the distributions of utility measurements. The linear interpretation of validity, along with requirements of a knowledge of base rates and selection ratios, suggests much greater promise for selection programs and personnel testing than would be assumed by most traditional interpretations of validity. In spite of this, no one seems to be asking questions to generate the metrics of performance assessments that we would need to be able to apply the Cronbach and Gleser utility model generally.

CRITERION-RELATED VALIDITY (N = 16)

Below we have listed one prototypical question concerning differential validity, one question concerning validity generalization (the opposite of differential validity) that appeared with a frequency of 1, and four questions concerning criterion-related validity that were not asked.

(1) Does differential validity exist for specific groups? (N = 5)

(2) Under what conditions is validity generalizable rather than situation specific? (N = 1)

(3) No questions asking if traditional methods of detecting differential validity (r_{xy}, $ß_{xy}$, $s_{y,x}$) are sensitive enough to detect expected differences.

(4) No questions asking about values implicit in "value-free" methods of evaluating selection tests as aids to decisions about applicants.

(5) No questions about relations between fairness and optimality.

(6) No questions about stability of validity across time.

The question about the extent to which we can expect validity to generalize across situations when statistical artifacts are removed effectively challenged the widespread assumption that the apparent lability of validity is due to differences in situations. When investigators asked if the observed variance in validity coefficients across situations for similar tests and jobs could be due to statistical artifacts rather than to situational differences, an innovative series of empirical, methodological, and theoretical investigations was immediately opened up.

It may be too early to conclude what the answer to the question about validity generalization will be. As with many innovative and important questions, the answer cannot be that validities are *either* generalizable *or* situation specific. Validities will very likely turn out to be generalizable to a degree, but judicious choices of situational characteristics, types of ability measure to be validated, and criteria of performance will bias the answer in one direction or the other. That the answer is complicated, however, does not gainsay the importance of asking the question.

The question about generalizability rather than specificity of validities should have stimulated questions about the sensitivity of different methods of detecting differential validity to expected variations of validity or regression equations within the range of differences one might expect as a result of variations in measurement bias in majority and minority samples. If, for example, the robustness of linear models, of which correlations are but an example, also implies an insensitivity to small to moderate differences between correlations, then analyses of sample sizes necessary to generate sufficient power must precede the asking of questions about generalizability.

The second unasked question listed above is, admittedly, a question that goes beyond our normal methods of studying effects of validities and errors of prediction on minority and majority-group hiring rates. In fact, such a question about our implicit values challenges us to defend explicitly the assumptions that we make when we evaluate selections tests by counting hits and misses (correct hires, correct rejections, false positives, false negatives) and summing our decisions across all members of our applicant pool. We may argue, if pressed, that counting hits and misses is objective and involves no value judgments. This argument lacks validity unless one is willing to argue that implicit values of −1 and +1 for misses and hits within all subpopulations in the applicant pool were generated by a utility analysis and do not represent value judgments. Lacking such utility evidence, the use of −1 and +1 weights across all subpopulations should be compared to other arbitrary weighting schemes to determine the effects on minority- and majority-group hiring rates, utility of the overall selection procedure, and explicit social and public policy goals. Once again, we cannot prejudge the outcome of the questioning. We can only note that the questions have not been asked.

The final unasked question listed above continues to emphasize our worries about our assumptions of stability of individual characteristics and relations between predictors and criteria across time. Without the questioning of the assumptions about stability, we will never raise the question about change across time.

RESEARCH ON GROUP PROBLEM SOLVING AND DECISION MAKING (N = 14)

We have listed below one prototypical question that was asked five times in the research studies on group problem solving, as well as two questions that were not asked.

(1) What structure, rules, procedures, or group characteristics enhance group problem solving? (N = 5)

(2) No questions about work in the year 2001 when work, particularly information-dependent tasks, may be done at home, alone, and not as a member of a group.

(3) No questions about interpersonal costs and benefits of working in a "group" who only communicate via computer terminals.

The importance of question 1 is obvious: As long as individuals in organizations are asked to function as committees and solve problems, it is important that we know the characteristics of such groups that contribute to the speed and quality of the solutions they generate.

The importance of the two unasked questions depends on our ability as predictors of the configurations and characteristics of organizations in the near future. If technological developments occur at a pace and in the directions we anticipate, the organizations of tomorrow may resemble only slightly the organizations of today. These anticipated technological developments have significant numbers of clearly intended consequences on task characteristics, input-to-output transformation processes, and predictability of effects on input materials of workers' efforts. Technological developments also have myriad unintended consequences on large numbers of organizational characteristics that may be only tangentially related to configurations of tasks and workflow.

For example, it may very well be true that many individuals work in formal organizations specifically because the "groupiness" of modern organizations may be a substitute for a lack of close social contacts and extensive social networks in their nonorganizational lives. Technological developments could easily alter this aspect of work organizations. The alterations and changes imposed by technological developments could have such extensive impacts on the social fabrics of formal work organizations that the next generation of organizations will be radically different from the organizations of today. It is one matter to accept the inevitable. It is quite another to accept it without conducting research to learn about its impact and what we can do to soften technological blows. If change is inevitable, we should learn enough so that we can relax and enjoy it.

LEADERSHIP THEORY (N = 11), ASSESSMENT OF LEADERSHIP PERFORMANCE (N = 18), AND DETERMINANTS OF LEADER PERFORMANCE (N = 37)

Leadership continues to be one of the enduring warhorses in the area of I/O research. The following list suggests that interest continues, almost unabated, in these studies.

(1) Do leader behaviors influence subordinate behaviors, vice versa, or both? (N = 5)

(2) How much of the variance in leader performance can be explained by

    (a) leader traits?

    (b) leader behavior?

    (c) the job/task?

    (d) organizational structure?

    (e) other structional characteristics?

    (f) implicit leadership theories of the observers? (N = 12)

(3) No questions about leadership in the year 2001 when face-to-face interactions between leaders and led may be zero.

(4) No questions about leadership in extremely high technology organizations.

Combining, as they do, an intellectual heritage from sociology and social psychology with the interest of I/O researchers in promoting the smooth functioning of complex organizations, these studies are fueled by a steady stream of inputs from social exchange theory, attribution theory, person/situation interactionism, Lewian field theory, and clinical psychology. The results, however, seem disappointing when measured against the benchmark of accounting for variance in the behavior of individuals in organizations or variance in organizational effectiveness. Considering the amount of research funds that has been spent on leadership research, this area may represent the largest unpaid promissory note in the history of I/O psychology. The returns do not seem commensurate with the financial and opportunity costs associated with the support. Whether this is a fair summary of the leadership area can, and obviously will, be challenged by some. Progress, however, has not been striking. Currently asked questions seem no more insightful nor built on a better data base than those asked ten or twenty years ago.

Tough questions are not being asked about differences in the meaning of the concept of leadership when applied to tank and bomber crews, railroad section gangs, insurance offices, data-processing departments, circulation departments of libraries, R&D laboratories, and academic departments. Distinctions between "supervision" and "leadership" provide a first approximation but are unlikely to do justice to the possible varieties of leadership, or differences in meanings of the concept of a leader, that are manifest in these different situations. It is one thing to hypothesize that different leader traits are differentially effective depending on the situation in which the leaders are functioning. It is quite another to assert, and then ask questions about, differences in the meanings of the basic concept that is being studied. At one level of an organization, for instance, we might find that successful leaders are those who establish contingencies between followers' behaviors and the outcomes the following desire. At other levels, leaders might be able to assume the desired behaviors are known and spend time and effort establishing needs in their followers for the rewards the leaders control and can distribute. The two processes are much different and are likely to generate interpersonal behavior patterns that are only vaguely recognizable as falling under the same general category.

ORGANIZATIONAL CHARACTERISTICS (N = 32)

Listed below are different combinations of independent and dependent variables that have been studied in the area of the influences of organizational characteristics on different aggregate measures of organizational functioning.

(1) What effects does organizational

    (a) size

    (b) technology

    (c) hierarchical structure

    have on

    (a) effectiveness?

    (b) intraorganizational conflict?

    (c) interorganizational relations? (N = 20)

(2) No questions about how macrocharacteristics are translated into individual responses.

Presumably, these different aggregate measures reflect, with different degrees of veridicality, behavioral tendencies of individuals in organizations. This assumption in turn implies there are mechanisms that translate these organizational structure properties into psychological responses. The translation mechanisms are little understood and seldom studied.

The alternative assumption, that aggregated organizational outcomes are independent of behavioral responses of organizational members, is, of course, interesting and perhaps should be seriously considered by researchers in this area. This assumption has much different implications for research by applied organizational researchers. Research questions that would be asked following this assumption would resemble the questions asked by sociologists, economists, and political scientists. Studies of organizations qua organizations devoid of people would be designed and their questions elaborated. Although the lines of research that would be pursued if this assumption were made would be foreign to many psychologists, it is likely that by making the opposite assumption and following the logic and conclusions, new ways of looking at both organizations and individuals would be generated.

The different combinations of antecedents and outcomes listed in the first general question above generate nine possible questions that, as a group, appeared some twenty times in our sample of articles. This is clearly a popular area to organizational researchers, but the questions seem curiously devoid of psychological information related to how individuals respond. The question, in its different forms and variations, seems analogous to "What are the effects of the shape of altimeter hands on the effectiveness of a bomber squadron? or "What are the effects of variations in the GNP across time on the job satisfactions of the employees of Herb's Cafe in Fort Worth, Texas?" In the case of the altimeter hands, the influence of one flight instrument from the many contained in a cockpit might be observable on a specific and narrowly targeted dependent variable; the altitude of any specific plane might be susceptible to such flight instrument variations. The mechanism of influence is clearly understood. Such a minute variation would be unlikely to have an observable influence on the effectiveness of an entire squadron; Its effects would be lost in the welter of error variance introduced by weather, pilots, and equipment other than altimeters.

Similarly, variations in GNP might influence the availability of other jobs in a labor market and also the amount of local unemployment, but probably would have only minimal observable influence on job satisfactions of specific individuals in the work force in a specific local area. The conceptual distance between GNP and individual affect seems too large to generate reliable effects. Models specifying links between GNP, the state of the general economy, local labor market conditions, perceptions of unemployment, and perceived alternatives available to workers have been constructed. The gross input-to-output relations are relatively uninteresting.

The general area of the influence of organizational characteristics on workers' responses is popular; studies are relatively frequent. The psychological theorizing and questioning that is necessary to study the mechanisms by which environmental characteristics are translated into psychological response tendencies has not been done. Actuarial studies are necessary first steps to map out the most fruitful areas for exploration. After the fruitful areas have been identified, as many indeed have been, the focus and the sharpness of the questions must be improved.

PERSONNEL DECISIONS (N = 13)

A typical question asked in the area of employment fairness and discrimination is:

(1) To what extent do stereotypes, race, or gender influence specific personnel decisions? (N = 6)

It is often studied in the context of the paradigm used to study attributions in social psychology. This consists of creating descriptions of pairs of individuals who are identical in all respects except on the attribute being studied — sex, race, ethnicity, ability, school attended — and asking a sample of individuals to role play personnel decision makers and make simulated hiring, promotion, or pay raise decisions about the simulated people. Although it is clear that these studies provide consistent data suggesting the operation of bias against blacks, females, and ethnic minorities, no one seems to be asking questions about the external validity of this laboratory behavior. In our creation of paper people in paper organizations, have we created the behavior we want to study? Do personnel decision makers, when faced with the nearly infinite variety of individual differences, use such irrelevant characteristics as sex or race to make important decisions about other individuals? The questions, however, must be asked in less contrived settings with greater promise of external validity.

UNIONS AND COLLECTIVE BARGAINING (N = 6)

As the list below suggests, unionization, collective bargaining, and other aspects of industrial relations subsystems of organizations are rarely studied by I/O researchers who publish in the five journals surveyed for this workshop.

(1) What determines an individual's union representation vote? (N = 1)

(2) What are collective attitudes of

(a) faculty?

(b) engineering/technical personnel?

(c) management?

(d) blue-collar workers?

(e) others toward collective bargaining and strikes? (N = 0)

The first question listed above was asked as a replication of research that had been conducted on approximately thirty union representation elections. The series of studies is innovative. Well-established theories of voting patterns developed by political scientists and social psychologists, theories of job satisfaction relating to behavioral patterns of individuals who experience dissatisfaction with different aspects of their jobs, and legal-judicial theories of influence on workers were combined into the study of how events that occur during a 30-day election campaign in an NLRB-sponsored election influence workers' voting behavior.

Studies such as these are important because they represent explorations by psychologists into areas that have not been considered important or fruitful areas of inquiry — at least they have not been areas that have occupied our attention to any significant degree. Choice behavior, particularly choice of third-party representation in an industrial relations system, is an area to which psychologists can make important contributions.

The questions above also indicates that when studies are conducted in the area of unions and industrial relations systems, they are not devoted to asking simple questions that will enable us to generate descriptions and tabulations of individuals' attitudes toward important characteristics of the industrial relations area. A broad data base is not being established from which one could launch more definitive and innovative studies that are based on carefully established empirical trends.

Industrial relations and unions are areas of applied organizational research in which the results have the potential for significant impacts on public and social policy. Intervention procedures such as final-offer abritration and binding arbitration for impasse settlements, as well as participants' views of industrial judicial procedures, must be studied in a variety of laboratory and field settings so that the policy decisions that may be imposed on public-sector, collective-bargaining agreements and conflict resolution procedures are generated from the best possible theory-based data. This area is not important simply because public policies are likely to be implemented. Research is important because collective bargaining represents a very convenient combination of theories of group conflict, procedural justice, and negotiation with the need to generate data that are applicable to immediately pressing policy considerations. Both the background research noted in the nonasked questions listed above, as well as innovative questions about negotiating as representatives of entrenched parties or why professionals honor picket lines, need to be explored.

MOTIVATION (N = 20)

One frequently asked question that appears in many forms in motivation research studies is:

(1) Does expectancy theory predict . . . ? (N = 5)

This question and others similar to it about other cognitive motivation theories are important. They are attempts to establish general empirical linkages between constructs assessed as part of theoretical networks and organizationally relevant behaviors. Verification of each tested hypothesis adds support to our theoretical interpretations of internal and external influences on behavior. Eventually, we will establish a network of relations rich enough that many of the present controversies and pseudo-controversies can be either resolved to shown to be empty of either theoretical or practical import. It is likely that such a step-by-step process that seeks to establish extensive networks will eventually succeed. If the theoretical constructs and the networks of relations are sufficiently robust to account for appreciably large amounts of variance in important behaviors, then the research strategy will have been successful. At the same time, we have in the area of motivation a much-researched and long-recognized problem in which researchers are still equating behavior with motivation and seeming to forget the lessons of multiple, converging operations. We have motivational techniques without firm theoretical bases being proposed as *theories* of motivation, and in general we have conceptualizations of motivation ranging from motivation as an energizing force to motivation as simply the consistency that is found in the stimulus-response connections that can be observed among individuals. Diversity and divergence are normally a sign of vitality in an area. In some cases, it may also be the disintegration preceding death or the lack of integration of knowledge because of a dearth of basic questions about the meaning of the construct as applied in a specific setting.

WITHDRAWAL BEHAVIOR (N = 14)

Turnover/absenteeism has been studied frequently in our immediate past and, although extrapolating from two data points is dangerous, this appears to be increasing in popularity.

(1) What (besides job satisfaction) are important antecedents of turnover and absenteeism? (N = 9)

Questions were all phrased from point of view of institution.

Speculation about reasons for the continuing interest are unlikely to be fruitful. What might be more fruitful would be to note that all of the investigators studying turnover seem to be phrasing their questions and designing studies from the perspective of organizations or institutions and not from the perspective of individuals who terminate or are absent. This one-way view of the behavior implies an organizational perspective that may narrow the focus of our questions very seriously.

These one-way views of the turnover process have provided us with ample insights into why people decide to participate or withdraw from a focal organization. The studies suggest that individuals are obviously avoiding an unpleasant work situation if there are alternatives available. Once the individual has left an organization, we normally have no information about continued participation in the work force, what attracts an individual to another job with a different organization where the work may be the same, or even what advantages individual employees report for having terminated working for a particular company. This view of departing personnel that stresses what they are leaving rather than what might be attracting them away also, unfortunately, adds to the view of the I/O researcher as one interested in problems from a management perspective. Asking questions and learning more about the allures and attractions of changing jobs, employers, and geographical regions might help us simultaneously learn more about what keeps individuals rooted on one job and organization for extended periods of time.

Still a third perspective on participation in organizations would be to ask questions about the values and motivations of those who choose voluntarily never to participate in formal work organizations on a full-time or semipermanent basis. Just as the study of work values of employed people provides us with insights into these individuals' behaviors in organizations, the work values of such peripheral "workers" as surfers or ski bums who may work only enough to meet their minimal requirements, temporary workers who show up at the temporary work dispatching office two or three days each week, or semipermanent drop-outs and drifters may provide us with a better perspective from which to view our more frequently studied populations. We may learn more about participation and withdrawal by studying nonparticipants than by studying their opposite numbers.

TRAINING (N = 7)

The following are the questions asked in the general area of training.

(1) Questions about how to design training methods. (N = 2)

(2) Questions about how well specific training methods work. (N = 3)

(3) Questions about how training should be evaluated. (N = 2)

(4) No questions about best training methods for special (hard-core unemployed) groups.

We have already commented on the overall lack of attention to this area in terms of its importance as a selection procedure. We also note the lack of attention to designing training methods for groups of individuals for whom traditional procedures have not been successful in the past. Educational research suggests that the search for innovative training methods for special groups may be more successful than the apparently fruitless search for differential validity. Such studies need to be attempted; the relevant questions must be asked.

GOAL SETTING (N = 13)

The following indicates the frequency of questions in the general area of goal setting as well as noting the specific questions asked.

(1) Does goal difficulty/specificity influence behavior? (N = 3)
(2) No questions about why subjects accept assigned goals.

Perhaps because of the curious habit of excluding study subjects who do not accept the goals they were assigned, we did not encounter fundamental research questions about why people should or do accept the goals they are assigned. Such questions, including such variations as how to increase goal acceptance among militant labor union members following a bitter strike, are needed before wide-scale implementation of supervision by goal setting is carried out.

DISCUSSION

We have discussed only a sample of the questions noted in Table 1.1. We have commented on the assumptions that seem to have been made implicity before the questions were asked. We have also noted many questions that were not asked but perhaps should have been. How do we now proceed from this listing and annotation to prescriptions that will lead researchers to ask more innovative questions? Perhaps we cannot; that might be expecting too much. At the same time, it seems obvious that we are not asking the innovative questions in our research that we should be asking.

One approach used in this exercise to analyze the questions being asked was to question the assumptions that were implicit in the study. "What is the best method to reduce halo in ratings?" suggests "Why do we want to reduce halo?" Questions were phrased in the negative. "Under what conditions do leader characteristics contribute to group performance?" becomes "Under what conditions does group performance proceed independently of the leaders?"

Phenomena previously regarded as sins caused by defects in investigators should be regarded, at least on a trial basis, as virtues. "Unreliability or instability of measurement over time is bad" becomes "Instability over time tells us something important about individuals" or "What part of temporal instability is true change and what is measurement error?" "Lack of homogeneity among items (KR-20 or Cronbach's alpha) is bad" becomes "High item homogeneity is bad. It reflects a collection of items with a great deal of measurement bias in common and tells us more about the habits of item writers than it does about the respondents." Each of these negatively phrased questions or sins regarded (temporarily) as virtues seems to open up more innovative studies than do the more conventional questions.

Accepting our fixed creeds without question often seems to impell us toward the routine rather than toward innovation — regardless of the truth of the creeds. "Parametric, systematic research is good" is one of our often voiced creeds. Asking questions about two new cells or conditions in a standard design to extend the range of varibles that have been studied, parametric though it may be, is not an example of innovative research or of what is meant by good parametric research. Neither is asking if another personality or need measure will moderate the often studied relation between job satisfaction and performance — either in its pristine or moderated form. We often praise such parametric studies by reiterating our creeds without thinking about the implications of our research questions. Note also comments on included in the section on Other Job Attitudes.

When other old certitudes and fixed creeds are inverted, "Traits are fixed and stable" becomes "Traits, just as any other set of skills and abilities, are changeable, trainable, and dynamic." "Validities are fixed by the jobs and abilities measured" becomes "Validities will change over time because abilities change through transfer of training."

Another of the truths that we cling to with a Promethean passion is that we need more longitudinal research studies. At first examination, this seems unassailable. If we want to move from studies of static input/output relations in which the black box of the individual or organizations remains inviolate, we must begin studying processes and changes as they occur across time in individuals or organizations. However, to ask even reasonable questions, without requiring that they be innovative, assumes that others have previously asked questions that inform us about the time periods across which one should study organizational phenonema. The study of life cycles of plants, animals, and other intact organisms can generally proceed in an orderly fashion. We have a carefully established data base that is informative about the life cycles, developmental periods, growth spurts, and life expectancy. We have no similar data base in I/O research from which to launch our sound and innovative longitudinal research questions. Without the data, questions based on sound hypotheses and innovative studies of important processes and developments are likely to generate inconclusive results because we chose a time period that is either too short for the phenomenon to be observed or so long that the process occurred and the organization or individual returned to a preexisting steady state leaving little trace of the process we wanted to study. Innovation is important and must be pursued. But innovation in content and theory questions about change and process cannot occur independently. We need either data from which to make empirical inferences about time cycles or a well-developed theory of organizational time that is not artificially imposed by business or academic year cycles that operate independently of the organizations we want to study.

There is a fine line, but a line nonetheless, between stating useful truisms and studying carefully their implications and stating and studying nonquestions. "Behavior is a function of the person and the environment" is a truism. It could not be false. What else could behavior be a function of? But, studying which characteristics of each account for variance in a variety of responses made by individuals is an important part of our discipline. "Men are different from women" is a truism. Industrial engineers, however, will testify that it is important to know precisely how they differ if one is to design equipment that can be used by both or used optimally by one group rather than by the other. Asking whether environmental or individual characteristics account for more variance is a nonquestion just as is asking about job preferences between men and women without asking about the specific causes of the differences. The answer to the first question probably will not generalize. The answer to the second, without the study of the causes, is trivial.

We have also tried in a limited way to be futurists and to envision some characteristics of organizations that will be changed in ten or twenty years. What will happen to work groups? Will supervisors interact face-to-face with their subordinates? How will computer terminals and phone lines change the nature of information and service organizations? Can we generalize from railroad gangs, insurance offices, and libraries to high technology organizations? When it is easier to disable a battleship or an aircraft carrier by knocking out the main-frame computer than by destroying the engines, we may be facing a generation of large and small organizations to which little of what we know will generalize.

Finally, we note the depressing frequency of the number of questions that were stimulated by others' research and by previously asked questions. Few were generated by researchers observing work organizations and workers first hand. Before one studies the temporary work industry, for example, one should perhaps "shape-up" at the local temporary service dispatching office. Talking with, not interviewing or giving assignments to, blue-collar or clerical workers is an activity that might produce research questions that have not been asked before. If they tell us that our job, studying them and their jobs, must be a pretty terrible way to make a living, we might learn something about both parties in the process.

Research on modern organizations is just as untidy and complex as organizational behavior is. Old truths and certitudes still work, but less often now than they did in the past. If we have learned anything from our past research, it should be that expecting or searching for a perfectly symmetrical, significant, meaningful, and clean result from one of our questions is a bit like expecting honesty and candor among politicians: One can always hope but we should also expect frequent disappointments. However, the more we can structure our research questions to both take advantage of what we already know and to avoid repetitions of past questions that may have been trivial to begin with, the more likely it is that our research efforts and question asking will generate important and useful information.

In documenting the realities of work in organizations revealed by our data, we need to know what we are doing. Our standard approaches and questions may be creating what we learn. We must avoid creating too many lies to document too few truths. We must question our questions. We have tried to provide a starting point to do this, an opening wedge. It is not enough to argue that the standard questions being asked are not innovative. Even if one could argue convincingly the alternative forms of the questions provided in this chapter are more innovative, this does not mean we have a valid algorithm that will transform routine into innovation. If questions generated in new areas by investigation following from these exhortations are noticeably divergent from past practices, this will have been a fruitful exercise.

2

What Research Questions Should We Be Asking?
A Survey of Opinion

☐ So far we have tried to describe the kinds of research questions that the field *does* ask, as reflected in a sample of the published literature. We thought it would be informative to contrast this information with some systematic sample of opinion as to what kinds of research questions *should* be asked. Are there large disparities in the content of the two sets of questions? That is, do people think we should be following much the same course as we have been or should we be striking off in new directions? Where should the energies and resources of the field be committed in the years ahead? What are the most crucial questions that should be answered? Similarly, are there differences in form between the way research questions are framed for published research and the way they are stated when advocating future research? Are the identifiable characteristics of such questions that it would be helpful to avoid? Do specific suggestions for future research exhibit special strengths that the published literature does not possess?

To help answer these questions we surveyed, by mail, approximately 14 per cent of the membership of the Division of Industrial and Organizational Psychology of the American Psychological Association (APA). The Division of I/O Psychology (Division 14) has approximately 1700 members. To qualify as member of Division 14, people must be members of APA, their Ph. D. dissertation must have been psychological in content, and they must have demonstrated significant interest in studying adult behavior in organizations. The members are primarily university and college faculty, consultants, and professional staff in public and private organizations. To the best of our knowledge, such a survey of the Division 14 membership has not been done previously.

This population was chosen because it was a feasible one to identify. It also includes a wider variety of behavioral scientist than might be inferred from the title. A large proportion of the membership of the Division of I/O Psychology teach in schools of business and administration in programs usually designated as programs in organizational behavior. Also the Division's membership includes many individuals who are interested in applied research problems that are much broader than those related to the effective management of business organizations. Consequently, we believe that the results of surveying this population would be broadly applicable to work in applied psychology in general.

OBJECTIVES

The aims of the survey were:

(1) to identify the research areas that division members think are most important and which they think should be given the highest priority;

(2) to compare these opinions of what *should* be done with a con-concomitant analysis of what *is* done, as indicated by the content analysis of journals reported in Chapter 1; and

(3) to identify, if possible, characteristics of the way research needs are stated that might either facilitate or hinder the subsequent development of specific research questions and/or projects.

METHOD

SAMPLE

A sample of 220 people was selected from the 1980 membership register of the Division of Industrial and Organizational Psychology. The sample was not a random one. It was "picked out" by the current authors so as to overrepresent the more active researchers in the division and to ensure that people working in academia, industry, private consulting organizations, private research organizations, and governmental organizations were all represented. Approximately 20 percent of the sample also are members of the Academy of Management and an attempt was made to give both departments of psychology and organizational behavior programs in business schools substantial representation.

While we do not claim to know everyone in the division personally, the major job activities of almost everyone, except those in the very youngest cohort, were familiar.

The survey was mailed in July of 1980 and one follow-up mailing was made after approximately 6 weeks. A total of 105 survey forms were returned, all of which were usable, in some form or other.

THE SURVEY FORM

Using essentially a blank piece of paper, respondents were simply asked to describe what they believe to be the most important research needs facing applied psychology as it is focused on adult behavior in organizations. It was suggested that each respondent identify from one to six research needs, but any number was certainly all right. Appeals were made to the respondents' altruism, commitment to the field, and selfish desire to change things. The survey cover letter is included in Appendix B.

Analysis

When the survey forms were returned they were edited slightly (for clarity) and each distinct suggestion was typed on a 5 × 7 index card. One of the authors (Campbell) then read through the entire stack three times to: (a) develop a reduced list of all the unique suggestions and (b) identify the principal themes that seem to characterize the content of the suggestions. Also, the cards were sorted and counted a number of different ways, as will be described below.

RESULTS

The 105 respondents produced a total of 454 suggestions. Not all of the suggestions had to do with suggestions for research. In some respect or other, almost everyone used the survey to comment on the state of the field, describe our worst faults, point an aggressive finger at deficiencies in our graduate education, complain about our mixed-up values, express optimism or pessimism about the future, and so on. In short, it was an opportunity to express strong feelings and beliefs, as well as to respond to a survey, and many people seized the opportunity.

Perhaps one example will be illustrative of the level of feelings that were expressed.

The first fifty years or so of industrial psychology seemed to be characterized generally by application of rigorous objective/scientific methdologies from the discipline of psychology to "real" problems as they occurred in business, industry, and government. The addition of a so-called organizational concept seems to have opened the door to sloppy, ill-considered, or even nonexistant research methodology. A whole body of sound research concepts seems to have been suppressed; e.g., reliability of measurement, power of statistical tests, adequate and well-thought-through sampling designs. . . . Unfortunately, a not uncommon phenomenon in the literature today is a "study" in which the authors sent a nonpretested, nonscaled questionnaire to a convenience sample of uncertain nature in which little or no thought was given to the reliability of the measurement or the meaningfulness of responses. Nonetheless, numbers are obtained and are subjected to the staggering array of sophisticated computer-assisted statistical techniques and "results" are obtained and generalized to a population of which the initial sample had very little relationship.

The above sentiments do not necessarily reflect the opinions of the authors. There were equally strong tirades against the perceived overconcern with individual differences and measurement to the exclusion of any acknowledgment at all that learning and motivation, as they operate through the organizational context, may influence behavior. Permit us one more example.

Too many people believe that the only science in industrial organizational psychology is using tests of primary mental abilities to predict job performance criteria and analyzing the resulting correlations with the most mathematically sophisticated multi-variate techniques possible. Don't these folks know that motives, attitudes, and other such soft-headed notions have a long history of scientific development in psychology? Get your head out of your trait/criterion correlations. People are profoundly affected by their environments. To ignore such a truism is to worship ignorance.

In our view such dissatisfaction is healthy. As long as people keep challenging each other there is hope for applied psychology.

TABLE 2.1   Initial Card Sort into Major Categories of Suggestions

Category	Frequency
Concrete substantive suggestions specific enough to offer some substantive guidance (for better or worse) for the field.	146
Nominations for very general topics, samples, or organizations to study.	248
Suggestions for how I/O psychology should improve itself.	32
Other suggestions or comments.	28
TOTAL	454

THE INITIAL CARD SORT

In addition to the non-research-oriented comments, many of the substantive suggestions were so brief or so general (e.g., "aging should be studied," "productivity should be investigated," "better criteria should be developed") that their potential for giving guidance to other people in the field is virtually nil. Consequently, an initial sort was made to divide the total number of cards into several categories corresponding to (a) relatively concrete substantive suggestions, (b) very general statements of possible research areas (e.g., productivity), possible samples (e.g., young workers), or possible sites (e.g., nontraditional organizations), (c) suggestions for how I/O psychology can be improved, and (d) other kinds of comments, complaints, and suggestions. The results of the frequency count are shown in Table 2.1.

The nature of the suggestions that were judged too brief is illustrated in Appendix C, in which they are simply listed.

SOME PRODUCTIVE CONFLICTS?

In the course of reflecting their opinions, the respondents came down on both sides of the fence on a number of issues. To

FIGURE 2.1 Conflicting Positions Within the Division 14 Sample

Side One	Side Two
A$_1$ Research should be carried out in a theoretical context and should be directed at theory testing.	A$_2$ We have too much "theory" in I/O psychology. We need to go after ecologically important (i.e., practical) questions.
B$_1$ We need broader, more generally applicable theory.	B$_2$ We need narrower, more detailed theories that are appropriate for specific domains of behavior.
C$_1$ Descriptive studies are bad. They pile up uninterpretable data and do not lead anywhere.	C$_2$ Descriptive studies are good. We have very little knowledge of the behavior we are trying to research.
D$_1$ There is too much emphasis on "measurement" for "measurement's" sake.	D$_2$ There is too little emphasis on valid measurement. The field is replete with lousy, unvalidated measures.
E$_1$ Research should focus on the processes within the individual or group that describe the causal sequences. We need understanding, not prediction.	E$_2$ Research should focus on important outcomes as dependent variables. That is, we must try to predict and explain the bottom line.
F$_1$ An information, processing (cognitive) model is our best foot forward.	F$_2$ A functional, behavioristic stimulus control approach will pay the biggest dividends.
G$_1$ Perhaps capitalism is not the only value system in which we should do research. For example, what happens if we take a Marxist perspective?	G$_2$ The U.S./capitalist/profit incentive system is the value system within which we should work.
H$_1$ Organizations are dehumanizing institutions.	H$_2$ The quality of the people in the work force is declining sharply.
I$_1$ We have learned virtually nothing about organizational behavior.	I$_2$ We actually know quite a bit, and some questions have been substantially answered, to the extent that they can be answered.

anyone who listens at all to what goes on in the field this should not be surprising, but it may be useful to list the major conflicts that the respondent comments seem to incorporate. They are shown as Figure 2.1.

Some of these dichotomies seem highly intercorrelated. For example, one gets the impression from reading the responses that someone who thinks there is too much "theory" in the field also wants more emphasis on measurement, more descriptive research, research on outcomes, and a behaviorist orientation. However, these data cannot be used to examine these speculations directly and readers should feel free to profile themselves.

Certainly, there are probably more such dichotomies in the field than were reflected in the survey results. However, one can ask whether all, or any, of these represent true conflicts or whether they would disappear if we had a better understanding of the role that theory and measurement should play, a more explicit realization of the purposes to be served by a particular piece of research, and a more realistic expectation of what is possible. We tend to think so. For almost all these dichotomies, both sides are true under a given set of circumstances and the fact that such conflicts appear to arise is most likely the result of our naivete.

AN OUTLINE OF RESEARCH NEEDS

The categories used in the content analysis of the published literature were used to categorize the 146 substantive research suggestions provided by the survey respondents. They are portrayed in Figure 2.2.

To keep the list manageable, the individual items were rewritten in some what briefer form than the original responses although we tried to preserve the original level of generality/ specificity in the response. The majority of the suggestions were mentioned only once and a frequency distribution across items or categories would be so skewed that there is little point in presenting it. Because so few suggestions were mentioned more than once the list still contains 106 entries. The few high-frequency items that were evident had to do with:

(text continues p. 70)

FIGURE 2.2   A Taxonomy of Research Needs Generated by the Survey of Division 14 Members

A. Job analysis
- The various job analysis methods should be compared.
- We need to develop an automated system for gathering job task data and funneling it into other activities.
- What are the similarities or differences between public and private managers?
- How can we measure the "comparative worth" of jobs?
- We still need a comprehensive taxonomy of job tasks and task requirements.

B. Recruitment
- Must study the effects of the "baby boom" demographics.

C. Criteria and individual performance measurement
- How can different levels of task "mastery" be defined and assessed?
- Who is the better evaluator of someone's performance?
- How can the feedback properties of performance appraisals be improved?
- Is feedback or evaluation better served by performance appraisal?
- What is the construct validity of self-evaluations?
- We must further develop the dollar criterion.
- Better anchors should be developed for behaviorally anchored rating scales.
- We must develop new methods for measuring the *utility* of individual job performance.

D. Selection/prediction
- Work samples should be developed that would serve as tests for the cognitive abilities needed in various jobs.
- What are better methods for testing the handicapped?
- We need more developmental research on computer-based testing.
- How can we better use personality and interest variables in selection?
- What is the construct validity of job previews?

(continued)

FIGURE 2.2 Continued

- Are assessment centers worth the cost?
- What types of organizations moderate the validity of biographical data used as predictors of job performance?
- Can we use physiological measures in personnel selection?

E. Turnover/selection
  - What are the *consequences* of turnover and absenteeism for the individual?
  - How can we move people *out* of organizations?
  - What are the psychological effects of unemployment?

F. Fairness, discrimination, and EEO issues
  - How do affirmative action programs affect the attitudes of current employees?
  - How do affirmative action programs affect the attitudes and performance of the people selected?
  - How does affirmative action affect the *skills* and *abilities* of people?
  - How can pay discrimination be eliminated?
  - What are the physical requirements of jobs, as they pertain to male/female differences?
  - How can we generate power for women and minorities?
  - Why do females frighten males at work?
  - Is biographical data appropriate for selection of minority group applicants?
  - How can the "fairness" of performance appraisals" be improved?

G. Aging/retirement/transfer
  - How can people be helped to cope with retirement?
  - What is the impact of job relocation?

H. Career development
  - We need to establish longitudinal data banks that collect information on all the educational, job, and career choices people make.
  - How can we give people a more sophisticated view of career opportunities?

FIGURE 2.2 Continued

- We should study career paths of people in minority groups.
- How can transition to a second career be facilitated?

I. Design analysis and research methods
- The construct validity of survey questions should be determined.
- How can research results be made more useful for policymakers?
- More cost/benefit analyses of interventions/programs should be conducted.
- We need more sophisticated methods of meta-analysis and more meta-analyses of existing literature.
- We need normative/descriptive studies on a variety of issues.

J. Individual training and development
- Need studies contrasting "hard core" individuals who "make it" versus those who do not.
- How can we upgrade the "marginally" employable?
- How can supervisors for minority subordinates be better trained?
- What are the most useful interviewing skills?
- How should we train supervisors to deal with alcoholics?
- How should people be retrained, and when?
- How can managerial decision making be improved?
- What influences self-esteem?

K. Evaluation of individual training and organization development
- What elements enhance the success of survey/feedback?
- Need more validation of organization development methods.
- How can we keep managements from buying fads?
- How effective is mixed discipline consulting?
- How can the use of industrial and organizational psychology interventions be facilitated?

(continued)

FIGURE 2.2 Continued

L. Motivation
  - How can "feedback" be made a permanent part of organizational practice?
  - When do employees feel they are being optimally utilized and how do their views on this issue differ from management's?
  - How does inflation affect perceptions of pay and pay increases?
  - We need more descriptive studies of the psychological contract.
  - How can people adjust to a job from which they can go no higher?
  - What are the specific consequences of using aversive controls in work settings?
  - We need longitudinal studies of how incentives and control systems affect productivity.
  - How can people on public assistance be induced to train themselves.
  - How can service occupations be given higher status?
  - How can we enhance individual *pride* in jobs?
  - What causes responsible behavior?

M. Effects of work on family life
  - We need studies of two-job or dual-career families.
  - How do bad experiences at work affect home life?

N. Attitudes and values
  - How do the values of top management affect policy/practice?
  - Why do subordinates tolerate unethical and dishonest bosses?
  - About what issues does management feel most powerless?
  - Study effects of media portrayal of work.
  - How to reduce materialistic values.
  - What are the correlates of job satisfaction?
  - How do job and life satisfaction correlate?

FIGURE 2.2 Continued

O. Job redesign/technological change
  - How will robot assembly methods affect the rank and file?
  - How do word processors affect clerical personnel?
  - How can changes that are made (e.g., job redesign) be institutionalized?

P. Leadership
  - We should study differences in male versus female leader behavior.
  - What are the consequence of different styles of delegation?
  - Better descriptions of leader behavior should be developed.
  - How does authoritarian leadership affect subordinate mental health.
  - What are the interactions of power, personality, and leader style?
  - What are the implications of transformational versus transactional leadership?
  - What non-supervisor-mediated controls will control subordinate behavior?
  - How should we select supervisors who must train new employees?

Q. Cognitive processes
  - We need descriptive research focusing on the cognitive processes of raters, survey respondents, and so forth.
  - The field needs better methods for studying the cognitive processes of managers.
  - How are performance judgments formed?
  - How do managers react to overload created by management information systems?

R. Communication
  - What makes "communication" effective?
  - What individual differences interact with specific communication needs?

(continued)

FIGURE 2.2 Continued

S. Role conflict, ambiguity, and stress
- We should study work as an "antidote to" and not a "cause of" stress.
- How should job stress be measured?

T. Collective bargaining and union membership
- What is the full range of formal and informal "grievance" procedures that people use in organizations?
- How can we improve bargaining processes (i.e., face-to-face group interaction)?

U. Organization structure and design
- Is a matrix structure better than functional/bureaucratic models? When?
- How should organizational effectiveness be measured?
- What is the correlation of organization level with prescribed versus discretionary job content?
- What management skills are needed at different organization levels?
- How does organizational climate relate to organization success?
- We should do critical incident studies of successful versus unsuccessful organizations.
- How do the observed consistencies between organizational structure and organizational practices arise?
- How does physical distance between units affect management?

(a) the effects of affirmative action policy on individuals,

(b) using an information-processing approach for studying management decision making and/or performance rating,

(c) the consequences of aversive control,

(d) the use of feedback to train and motivate,

(e) the development of better measures of organizational effectiveness, and

(f) the comparison of alternative job analysis methods.

"High"-frequency items would be those mentioned three to five times. Keep in mind that the original responses judged to be too brief or too general are not included in these frequency counts.

SOME GENERALIZATIONS BASED ON SURVEY RESPONSES

In general, the responses were not as "meaty" as one might hope and those who seek substantial substantive direction will be disappointed. Perhaps the survey format was *totally* responsible for this, but we fear not. To a considerable degree, in our opinion, the field does not have very well worked out ideas about what it wants to do. There was relatively little consensus about the relative importance of substantive issues.

The above aside, what do these responses seem to say about how well we formulate research questions, what we do right, what we do wrong, what boxes we might be getting ourselves into, and where we seem to be heading? Given the simplemindedness of the survey, making such inferences is probably risky. Nevertheless, here they are.

(1) Although a few of the responses suggest that some individuals have not kept up with the literature very well, the predominant impression is that people are well aware of what is published and are very dissatisfied with it. A very negativistic theme runs through out the respondent comments. The chief complaints were about the lack of "practicality" in the published literature and its elitist nature (i.e., an overemphasis on theory, complex design, and complex analyses). We perhaps would agree. There frequently does seem to be an overemphasis on theory and multivariate methods as ends in themselves. Explicit consideration of how the answer to a research question will be of value is often neglected.

(2) Although very few in number, some of the survey responses talked about research questions that probably already have been answered, *given what is possible to do*. It is this last

phrase that we think deserves more attention. Consider the following two examples of survey responses.

> Why is job proficiency so unexplainable? A cross-validated R^2 of .50 is virtually unheard of in personnel selection, but even at that degree of association, half of the variance of performance remains unexplained. Why?
>
> How much difference does a use of selection tests make in performance? Do correlations of .35 and a selection ratio of 50 percent or 75 percent justify the use of tests?

In our opinion, the questions stated, or implied, in these responses have already been answered about as well as we can expect them to be without some drastic change in the way organizations do business. The danger here is that we feel eternally inadequate because we cannot produce perfect predictions about individuals on perfect criterion metrics. Further, if the people in the field make the error of implying that something close to perfection is possible, if only we were not so stupid, then others (e.g., managements, courts of law) might decide to hold us to such levels of perfection. It is a corner that we should not get ourselves into.

(3) The tendency to state research questions and research needs in such general terms is disturbing. Again it may be *entirely* a function of the survey format, but we do not think so. Such generality seems characteristic of our discussions about research in many contexts (conventions, classrooms, and so forth). We frequently seem not to recognize the need for greater precision or concreteness. For example, "summaries of the literature," on a topic often mix together studies that use very different dependent variables (e.g., job performance and self-rated effort in the motivation literature). As a result, we probably do not carry very accurate generalizations around in our heads. One implication is that the general research question an individual thinks is important and the specific question that is finally executed in a study may be so different that there is very

little connection between the two. Consider the following two examples.

> Given a clearly vital need to utilize the best talents at all levels of our society, I believe that the more accurate classification of people to jobs is of continuing importance. This effort could subsume the need to define and identify managerial talent.

> How can we structure organizations, develop leadership styles, and create climates that will promote involvement and interest of the organizational members, that will allow self-determination on the part of each member, and that will *not* foster the alienation that is so widespread (and destructive) in our organizations?

Neither gives much guidance about what kinds of research should be done. While two people could nod agreement regarding each statement, they also could then go and do very different things such that each would think the other was hopelessly off base. Every program of graduate training should probably include strong doses of drill and practice in "being explicit."

(4) Some of the survey responses seem to imply that it is possible to obtain, via research, general answers to general questions. For example, "Is training or selection more important?" "Who is the best evaluator of someone's performance?" "How should people be retrained?" "How can we move people out of organizations?" "Do OD methods work?" Stated in such a fashion, the questions become unanswerable and have very little heuristic value for researchers in the field. Many times it is not a matter of changing or refining the question. It should simply be avoided.

(5) The overuse of the questionnaire as a data collection device was generally damned to hell by the respondents. The spector of developing a science of questionnaire x behavior is too close for comfort for many people.

(6) Many questions are unanswerable, as posed, because their meaning is completely dependent on a number of parame-

ter values in a particular situation. A shopworn example is whether ability or motivation is a more important determinant of performance. The question is virtually meaningless because the answer is dependent on the way performance is defined and on the variability in ability and the manipulability of the motivational antecedents. Any answer can be found depending on what range of values for the parameters are chosen for study. Many of the suggested questions were of this form.

Perhaps one overriding issue to consider here is the question of what it would really mean if a particular theory were "supported" by research or a particular question were in fact answered at the same level of generality and in the same form as it was aksed. Precisely what would be gained, what would we then really know? Some of the suggested questions would lead to important generalizations and practical knowledge. Others seem to lead nowhere and to have few implications for anything. Somehow we must train ourselves to consider the consequences of asking a question in a certain way. Perhaps every researcher should seek out an especially candid devil's advocate and proceed through several cycles of a "what if" exercise. What if the study came out one way? What if it came out another? What if you asked 100 people in the field what the results will be good for? What if someone asks you what difference the results will make in your future research or practice? And so on and so on.

If people went through such exercises regularly, we do not think questions like the following would be asked.

> Empirical research is needed on the internal, external, construct, and statistical validity of various strategies of research on I/O problems: Lab experiments, controlled field experiments, action research, post hoc case studies of reforms, correlational studies, two-wave panel studies, etc. At present, we have only a scanty empirical basis for adopting one or another approach and for assessing the kind and degree of error that is likely to be involved.
>
> Should appraisal be evaluative or developmental?

COMPARISONS OF WHAT IS PUBLISHED WITH WHAT IS DESIRED

One of our principal goals in the project was to make some comparisons between the research questions that are addressed in the published literature and the research questions that the survey respondents thought should be addressed in the future. Obviously, we cannot make highly precise comparisons regarding the frequencies of specific kinds of questions and test the statistical significance of the differences. However, we do believe it is appropriate to comment on the qualitative distinctions between the two sets, the basic themes that seem to distinguish them, and the differences in values that seem to be reflected. Thus, while the following points are quite judgmental and they cannot be buttressed with precise frequency counts, they do seem like reasonable statements to make.

(1) The questions posed by the survey respondents have a much more applied flavor than does published research. They are less theory oriented and much more, almost exclusively, concerned with practical problems. Yet we swear an oath that well over half the sample were academics. There is little reason to believe that the authors of the journal articles examined in Chapter 1 and the survey respondents are sampled from qualitatively different populations. The survey sample was purposely selected to overrepresent individuals who do research and publish. Why then the strong qualitative difference between the two sets of research questions? One possible reason is that while it is easy to pose questions for future study, the actual research effort costs money and somehow the funding structure dictates a different kind of question asking. For example, applied research is more expensive and more difficult to "manage," as when attempting to secure timely subject cooperation and sponsor support. This makes it more risky for the individual investigator. Also, federal funding agencies have historically leaned toward support of basic rather than applied research.

Another explanation might be that the publication reward system is structured so as to promote getting a number of things published in a relatively short space to time. Perhaps grappling with applied problems is too risky for people whose performance is judged, at least in part, by how much they publish per unit time.

Finally, there may be some kind of shared value system within the field that says applied questions have lower status than more basic or theoretical ones. As a consequence, responding to an anonymous questionnaire is one thing, but putting your name on a publication is another.

While these speculations about causes may or may not be true, the difference in emphasis is indeed there. When advocating future research questions people would like to see much greater research emphasis on applied questions than is reflected in the published literature.

(2) The largest domain of published research in I/O psychology and organizational behavior has to do with the measurement of and understanding of so-called affective responses to jobs such as, job satisfaction, role conflict, role ambiguity, job commitment, job involvement, and feelings of job stress. Such topics are virtually *absent* from the need statements. Here again we swear that there was no conscious intent to exclude people from the survey sample who are interested in these kinds of questions. Again we can only offer speculation for why this result was observed. Perhaps these topics have simply run their course and interest in them has waned. Perhaps it is a function of the difference in level of generality between the survey responses and the questions incorporated in the published literature. For example, when a general question pertaining to motivation is translated to a specific researchable question perhaps even the survey respondents would be forced to resort to measuring affective responses. Finally, the publication reward structure may again exert a significant effect. That is, most of these topics are examined via the questionnaire as the principal research instrument. Questionnaires are relatively inexpensive, can be assembled quickly, can be used with large sample sizes, and make data analysis relatively easy. In cost/benefit terms doing

research on "affective responses" with questionnaires is an effective way to generate publications. Now, we are not trying to damn the entire enterprise or say that role conflict, job commitment, and other such variables should not be studied. However, we do believe that a reward structure that places such a premium on quick an inexpensive research for publication will have, and is having, negative consequences.

(3) The published literature contains a sizable chunk of research on research methods. The survey respondents did not mention this sort of thing all that often, except to complain bitterly about the overuse of questionnaires, and in one instance at least, to call for more work on meta-analysis. We do not worry about this point all that much. It is gratifying to note that when people in the field think of future research needs they think almost exclusively in terms of substantive issues. We are relatively confident that there will always be a significant number of people who do work on methodological issues as well.

(4) The survey respondents call for a far higher proportion of descriptive research than is found in the literature. They have a considerable need to know the extent of productivity problems, motivational problems, training problems, and so forth. Here the reasons for the difference seem relatively clear. Descriptive research has a lower status in academic circles than research that tests a model or tries to substantiate a prediction. Descriptive studies are viewed as less "scientific" or as not leading to useful generalizations. However, in their day-to-day work, applied psychologists and organizational behavior specialists have a great need for answers to a considerable number of descriptive questions. For example: For various entry level jobs, what proportion of the employees possess basic reading and arithmetic skills? What proportion of various types of supervisory jobs is composed of "leadership" behavior? What problems are created and/or solved by affirmative action policies? While it is certainly possible that certain kinds of descriptive questions can yield very little generalizable information, it is also true that the survey respondents feel a

strong need for filling in many gaps of our knowledge with descriptive studies. We tend to share their opinions. Descriptive studies do seem to have rather low status as research topics and a low probability of being submitted for publication and/or accepted for publication. This is in spite of the fact that many important organizational behavior phenomena are underdescribed and poorly measured. For example, we would put such things as leadership behavior, problem-solving behavior, motivational contingencies, and equity comparisons (i.e., Do people make them? When? With whom?) in this category. There is too quick a tendency to jump to theory testing and prediction.

(5) The need statements seem to worry more than the current published literature about the following topics.

- *The development of new selection methods.* This usually meant the development of alternatives to psychological tests.

- *The impact of management values on personnel practices and policies, individual motivation, and management decision making.* This topic was viewed as having suffered from extreme neglect in the past even though values are seen as having an important influence on behavior in organizations.

- *The impact of the job on the family.* The primary intent here was in the dual-job or dual-career family and on how it affects the work life and family life of both people.

- *The effects of inflation.* The respondents worried a fair amount about the new economy (i.e., unstable inflation and interest rates) and its effect on perception of pay equity, motivation, and job satisfaction.

- *Problems of career redirection, retraining, and retirement.* As a result of the more unsettled economic conditions and the even more rapid changes produced by high technology, the survey respondents see the need for more research on how to retrain people, redirect careers, and plan for a satisfactory retirement.

- *The effects of affirmative action.* Some respondents were worried about the possible negative effects of affirmative action on people already in the organization and on those who were selected under the auspices of an affirmative action program.

- *The motivational and cognitive processes involved in making performance judgments.* A cognitive information-processing approach to studying how people make choices among alternatives and how they judge the performance of others was the most frequently mentioned new area. Presumably this means that we should borrow concepts and procedures from cognitive psychology and apply them in the organizational setting.

- *The construct validity of questionnaire responses.* The suggestions in this category had a rather negativistic quality. Commensurate with the view that questionnaires are overused was the expectation that studies of the construct validity of self-report questionnaires would reveal their serious shortcomings.

- *Consequences of aversive control.* Some of the survey respondents wanted to see more empirical research regarding what "punishments" are used in organizations, and what their effects are.

- *Comparisons of alternative job analysis methods.* Given the increasingly important role of the job analysis in judgments about the validity of selection methods, several respondents called for more research on the usefulness of different job analysis methods for different purposes.

While they have a certain topical flavor, the items in this list represent substantive areas of research that are important and deserving of attention. We were particularly gratified to see an increased concern with the role of values. In our opinion, most of us do fully appreciate the role of values in our research.

CONCLUDING COMMENTS

In general, we (authors included) are not very articulate in how we talk about potential research questions. We believe this to be true even after discounting the constraints imposed by the survey format. The discourse tends to be at too general a level;

too many nonquestions creep in and the consequences that might result from trying to answer particular questions are seldom considered explicitly. If our ideas and conversations could somehow be made more precise we believe that our collective stereotypes about what we know and do not know would be become clearer and more useful.

People in the field are calling for more descriptive research, more investigation of applied problems, less reliance on the questionnaire method, more attention to the analysis of judgment and problem-solving processes, and a wider consideration of the role of value system and family considerations. To the extent that we can talk about these things in more precise ways without ending up with questions that have few meaningful consequences, we will make progress.

3

Research Needs from the "Real" World

☐ Besides surveying people within the field we were also interested in trying to describe needs that human resource managers and administrators believe to be the most pressing and important. That is, could we infer research needs from the way people in organizations described their most important human resource problems. The temptation here was to make all possible comparisons among (a) the published literature, (b) the survey sample, and (c) managers and administrators. Such comparisons might identify additional areas of needed research as well as alert us to additional pitfalls in the way research needs are identified and questions formulated.

Lacking the resources to do a major survey, we decided instead to gather a sample of human resource development reports, planning documents, and "white papers" that organizations had generated internally and that addressed the kinds of problems in which we were interested. For governmental and educational organizations these are public documents, but for private organizations they are not. We were able to obtain them only under the condition that sources would not be identified and only general trends would be reported.

We secured such documents from fourteen organizations, five public and nine private. In no sense do they constitute a random or representative sample of U.S. organizations. They obviously tend to be those organizations most prone to think systematically about human resource problems and to write down what they are thinking and planning. The sample is skewed further because we only approached those organizations where a contact person was known to us. Consequently, the sample is probably even more likely to consist of organizations that have used behavioral scientists and that have used applied research.

The written reports were supplemented by ten face-to-face or telephone interviews with managers and administrators who had significant human resource management responsibilities. Again, these individuals were in no sense representative of human resource management in the United States. They were a "convenience" sample in the fullest sense of the word.

Because of the obvious limitations in the above information, we cannot draw any firm inferences or make any precise comparisons. However, in spite of these limitations, we again believe that these data yield some generalizations that are well worth discussing. We do think they give the flavor of the major concerns organizations have and can be used to contrast what managements worry about, with what the survey respondents worry about, and with what is actually studied by the people who publish in the major journals. Some of them may seem obvious, but even in these instances perhaps we have been neglecting the obvious a bit too much.

SOME RESULTS

A portrayal of the need statements gleaned from management interviews, corporate planning documents, and public agency white papers is presented below. Although the frequencies for each item were necessarily small, some very general statements about relative frequencies of items are summarized in Figure 3.1.

Taken together the research needs talked about at the corporate and agency planning level are reasonably similar to the substantive concerns of the Division 14 sample. This is not too surprising since a number of the people who helped generate these reports are organizational behavior or industrial relations

(text continues p. 87)

FIGURE 3.1   A Taxonomy of Research Needs Generated from Management Interviews, Corporate Planning Documents, and Public Agency White Papers

A. Research that speaks to the description and/or diagnosis of human resource problems
- Descriptive studies designed to *identify* the primary human resource problems in the organization (e.g., asking middle management if there are problems in how top management communicates to them).
- How can employee motivational problems be identified?
- What new data bases would be the most useful for managing human resources?
- Need standardized methods for identifying training needs and developing training programs.
- How can important productivity problems be systematically identified?
- How can personnel information be optimally structured for automated data manipulation?
- How can we systematically monitor and describe the negative effects of management practices?
- How can we develop a "health records" data that would allow a better tracking of hazards, lost time, and so forth?

B. Recruitment/selection concerns
- How can we achieve fairness *and* usefulness in selection procedures?
- How can we better test for physical abilities?
  - As the result of advertised job openings, how do applicant pools form?

C. Concerns for individual and unit productivity
- How can the productivity of service personnel be better measured?
- How can so much lost time (e.g., absenteeism, long breaks, other time away from job) be prevented?
- How can measures of specific unit effectiveness be improved?

D. Retention/turnover problems
- How can the organization retain the people who should be retained?

(continued)

FIGURE 3.1 Continued

- What are the most equitable and least disruptive strategies for "work force reduction"?
- How can the problems of "relocation" (job transfer) to another site be minimized?
- What are the effects of management turnover, rotation, and the like on productivity, policy formulation, and so forth?

E. EEO concerns
- How can job evaluation methods be used to achieve equal pay for equal work?
- How can an organization get more women into management?
- How can *everyone* in the organization be sensitized to EEO issues?

F. Concerns for management and employee development
- How can interpersonal communication skills be improved?
- How can we best train foreign nationals at U.S. sites for jobs in their home countries?
- How should we deal with employees whose skills have become obsolete?
- How can an organization develop a career management system?
- What is the best way to teach "time management"?
- What are the important consequences of a leader or supervisor as a role model? How can modeling skills be improved?
- How can supervisory and management training be made more relevant to *specific* job concerns?
- How can the determinants of training needs and the development of basic training programs be made more systematic or even automated?
- What individual work problems can be helped by professional counseling?
- How can specific operational goal setting skills be taught to managers and supervisors?

FIGURE 3.1 Continued

- How can we develop managers as role models who:
  — act like they want subordinates to act;
  — are accountable;
  — are ethical;
  — face problems directly.
G. "Evaluation" research
  - Need evaluation research on highly marketed fads.
H. Concerns for individual motivation
  - Are young employees really "alienated"?
  - What will reward the new young employee so as to induce attendance, reasonable effort, and a modicum of job satisfaction and commitment to the organization?
  - Will flexible work schedules reduce absenteeism and improve productivity and satisfaction?
  - How can the commitment of the technical/professional employee be maintained?
  - How can people be induced to feel accountable for the work they do?
  - How can individual responsibilities and goals be made clearer?
  - How can appraisals be better used to give feedback, motivate, and compensate individuals?
  - As the result of decreased mobility (i.e., high cost of transportation, inflation, changing values), are the things people want from work changing?
  - How can appraisal, promotion, and training and development systems be made consistent in terms of their objectives, the feedback they provide, and the behaviors they reward?
  - What are the relative influences of group norms versus intrinsic rewards versus extrinsic rewards on behavior?
  - What are the negative and positive effects of centralized controls in military and public organizations?
  - How can identification and accountability, relative to organization goals, be increased?

(continued)

FIGURE 3.1 Continued

- We need more functional analyses of management behavior. For what are they *really* rewarded, punished, and so forth?

I. Problems pertaining to compensation practices
- What assumptions underlie current compensation practices and what is their validity?
- How does inflation change perceptions of pay and pay practices?
- What benefit systems are appropriate for the "new economy"?
- What benefit systems do employees value most?
- Can pay plans be used to promote higher productivity?

J. Concerns for unionization
- How can unionization of production and service personnel be prevented?
- How can white-collar unions be prevented?
- How can professional/technical unions be prevented?
- What alternative strategies will satisfy employee needs for "due process"?

K. Concerns for management policy and practice
- How can communication/feedback to all units from top management be facilitated?
- How can personnel allocation and classification be made more efficient?
- What are the "constraints" that managers/planners/other decision makers "perceive" as having serious effects on their behavior (i.e., laws, regulations, company policies, social constraints, and so on).
- Can the "real" efficiency of using a fluctuating work force (which attempts to minimize labor costs) versus maintaining a more "stable" work force (involving periodic surpluses and shortages) be compared?
- To what extent are decisions to maximize in the short run a problem? How can longer range goals be facilitated?

FIGURE 3.1 Continued

- Why is forecasting and planning behavior driven out? Or is it? How can it be facilitated?
- How can we better plan for baby-boom demographics (those born between 1945 and 1960)?

L. Implementing technological change
  - What are the best strategies for redesigning jobs?
  - How can all employees be kept current on new microelectronic equipment?
  - What will be the effects of microelectronic information processing equipment on clerical and management personnel?
  - Given personnel turnover, how do we transfer "ownership" of a personnel practice from the developer group to a new group that must continue to use it?
  - How can equipment changes best be implemented?

M. Concerns for safety and conservation
  - How can individual safety behaviors be promoted?
  - How can safety features of jobs and equipment be improved?
  - How can we teach and maintain individual behaviors that promote energy conservation in the organization?

specialists of one kind or another. However, besides the similarities there are also some differences and we think it is appropriate to list the following.

(1) There is a dominant concern with the *description* and *diagnosis* of human resource problems. It is stronger here than in the responses of the survey sample, which in turn was much stronger than the emphasis on such research in the published literature. Certainly this result was not unexpected. Also, we do not advocate that all behavioral science research in organizations shift to the descriptive mode. However, neither should the research-and-publication enterprise discourage it. It is

clearly a strongly felt need on the part of people in organizations.

(2) A concern for individual motivation pervades almost everything. It is the preeminent topic and is given far more emphasis than even the survey sample and the published literature give it. Organizations perceive themselves to have very serious problems in this area. Consequently, while researchers and academicians may disparage motivation as a useful concept, the problems it subsumes will not go away; and in fact, they are perceived as crucial by the people who must deal with them.

(3) The primary concerns of the survey sample and the published literature seem to be with independent variables (the criterion problem notwithstanding), while the people in organizations seem more concerned with the dependent variable (i.e., the problem to be fixed). For example, retention and productivity pervade much of the discussion about human resource problems, and were mentioned by every manager with whom we talked. The reasons for this difference in orientation may be quite understandable; however, its implications for research problem formulation are still worth pointing out. Very different research gets done if one has a favorite predictor treatment, questionnaire, or other independent variable and if the aim is to find a context in which to use it, try it out, or sell it, than if the initial concern is with a substantive problem regarding some organizational outcome and the aim is to develop an explanation or solution. Both good and bad, and both basic and applied, research can be done from both perspectives. Unfortunately, the former too often resembles the analogy to the little boy and the hammer (i.e., give the little monster a hammer and he will pound on everything in sight). Perhaps a higher proportion of our research should start with the problem and work toward a solution rather than searching for problems to fit solutions.

(4) Issues pertaining to pay and compensation are mentioned relatively more often here than by the literature or the

survey respondents. Again it is the motivational aspect that dominates. However, this topic is also dominated by a concern for how inflation, or the lack of economic stability, will affect compensation practices and individual perceptions of pay. The term "new economy" was used frequently.

(5) Evaluation research is mentioned hardly at all. This corresponds to the experiences of the authors to the effect that management seldom shows concern for the evaluation of training programs, organization development, and the like. Why this is so may incorporate a number of questions that would be worthwhile to study via research. Perhaps the cost/benefit ratio for evaluation research is not perceived to be favorable enough to warrant asking for it. If so, what is it that contributes to such judgments?

SUMMARY COMMENT

As would be expected, the concerns of administrators and managers translate into very practical research needs. While we certainly do not want to push everyone in the field up on a bandwagon of highly applied research (or any other bandwagon for that matter), it might be wise for researchers to be a bit more concerned with the dependent variable when formulating their research problems. The overriding concerns of human resource administrators and managers for description and diagnosis and for problems categorized as motivational in nature should make us pause and at least consider whether or not some of our research efforts should be redirected.

4

Antecedents and Characteristics of Significant and Not-So-Significant Organizational Research

☐   What is the process by which scholars become engaged in significant organizational research? How can a researcher identify innovative research projects that will result in a substantial increments to knowledge? These are difficult questions. They deal with the very essence of organizational research. Indeed, definitive answers to these questions may not be possible. Significant research may be the result of chance, or luck, or experience and judgment on the part of the scholar. Significant research projects may originate in the intuitive and idiosyncratic cognitive processes of investigators. The truth of the matter is that we simply do not know how "innovative" and productive investigators generate their innovative and productive research questions. Thus the purpose of this chapter is to face this dilemma directly and ask whether any identifiable patterns exist in the behavior of researchers themselves.

Understanding how we become engaged in significant research also means understanding how we become engaged in not-so-significant research; and a substantial amount of not-so-significant research is available for examination. A common criticism of industrial and organizational research is that it is dull. Research outcomes often are neither interesting nor sig-

nificant. The problems chosen for investigation often are
already well researched and trivial. In many respects the "Innovations in Methodology" conference was a direct response
to the abundance of insignificant research in the literature.

The notion of research significance affects us all. We have to
make choices about which research projects to undertake, and
our decisions often weigh the outcomes and publishability of
the final product. And of course after the research is undertaken, there are endless evaluations: by colleagues who read
drafts and provide criticisms; by journal referees; perhaps by
journal editors; by department heads; by promotion and tenure
committees; by readers of the journal; and by other scholars
doing research in the same field. Various devices are employed
to assess the research, including journal quality, number of
citations, and in some cases, the paper may even be read. We
are thus continuously involved in the evaluation of research
significance. While these evaluations are far from perfect and
provoke a great deal of uncertainty, there nevertheless does
seem to be enough agreement across people in the field about
what is significant and what is not to use this judgment as a
starting point for a study of the origins of significant versus
not-so-significant research.

The study described in this chapter had two goals. The first
was to compare directly significant and not-so-significant research along a number of specific dimensions. This comparison
may help us to outline the antecedent conditions of significant
organizational research. A better understanding of the possible
determinants of significant research may result. The second
goal of this chapter was to develop criteria for predicting significant research *in advance.* In other words, what should an
investigator look for when choosing a research project in order
to enhance the probability that it will make a significant contribution to knowledge. We approached this objective by ob-
taining a sample of investigators and by tracing some of their
research projects back to their origins. The antecedents of
significant research are something about which we know almost
nothing, and this is the activity we must begin to understand.

An "early warning" system of some sort may be necessary if we are to improve the significance of organizational research undertaken and eventually submitted for publication.

Good papers often are characterized by such things as good writing, novel ideas, a clever methodology, or the integration of different issues into a single study. These notions make sense, and two recent papers offer particularly useful perspectives about characteristics of research outcomes. To a considerable degree, these papers provide the conceptual framework for the study described here.

In 1971, Murray Davis, a sociologist, proposed an intriguing idea. He argued that sociological theories that have significant impact are those that are "interesting." Davis claimed that impact and significance have little to do with truth or empirical proof. Indeed, verifiable theories may be soon forgotten. A theorist or a piece of work is considered significant simply because the work is interesting.

To qualify as interesting, Davis said that the theory has to deny certain assumptions held by the audience. If all assumptions are denied, then the theory will be seen as unbelievable or irrelevant. If no assumptions are denied, the theory will be seen as obvious, as replowing old ground. The theory must be in the middle. The theory must differ moderately from the readers' assumptions in order to surprise and intrigue. From an analysis of sociological literature, Davis developed twelve propositions that described when theories would deny some assumptions of the audience and hence be perceived as interesting. Examples are theories in which the assumed independent variable in a causal relationship is shown to be a dependent variable, or where assumed covariation in a position direction between phenomena is shown to be in a negative direction, or when a phenomena that appears to be ineffective is shown to be effective, or that what seem to be unrelated phenomena actually are composed of a single underlying theme, or what seems to be bad is really good, and so on. Theories that have one of these characteristics will tend to be noticed and will have impact. If a study is simply designed to reaffirm the assumption set of the audience, then it is not likely to be very significant. Davis's contribution is that he went beyond the notion of "newness" in research, and described twelve explicit characteristics of research ideas that might be considered in advance.

The second paper that helped give us some perspective is a report of a study by Stephen Gottfredson (1978), who examined the peer evaluation system by collecting opinions about articles from nine different psychology journals. This was an empirical, cross-sectional study that included opinion ratings by 299 scholars on 83 statements describing attributes of journal articles. Gottfredson's study provided a comprehensive list of article characteristics, and the results indicated that judges are highly reliable when estimating the quality of articles. The 83 items were summarized in 9 scales. Key characteristics were called originality, stylistic/compositional qualities, ho-hum research, whether the paper provided direction for new research, and the type of substantive contribution.

The work of both Davis and Gottfredson dealt with evaluation after the fact. Their research attempted to explain the success of already published papers. One comes from sociology and one from psychology, one pertains to theories and the other to empirical papers, but when taken together these two papers provide a framework from which to begin exploring the antecedents as well as the characteristics of significant research. From this starting point we may be able to identify characteristics that suggest early on whether a project is likely to be perceived as original, whether it denies the assumptions of the audience, or whether it will most likely generate more ho-hum responses.

METHOD

The purpose of the study reported here was to develop a direct comparison between significant and not-so-significant research from two perspectives — characteristics of the research output, and the initial circumstances under which the research was undertaken. Thus we wanted to measure both antecedents and consequences. Learning about the research beginnings required personal interviews. Controlling for differences in research experience and creativity was also important so we adopted a "within-person" research strategy. Each investigator would be interviewed twice, once for a project considered significant, and once for a project considered not significant.

Sample and Procedure. The respondents were a convenience sample of 29 scholars. All of the participants in the Innovations in Methodology working sessions at CCL in Greensboro, August 1980, were interviewed. Additional researchers were interviewed at the University of Minnesota and Texas A&M University. The criterion for selection was that the scholar had done research and was recognized as a capable scholar, and had research projects that would be considered significant and not-so-significant.

Criterion of Significance. The first problem concerned the definition of significant and not-so-significant research. We decided to let the respondent select a research project in each category, using acceptance by colleagues in the field as the criterion. Investigators are aware of feedback in the form of acceptance by reviewers and colleagues, citations, and whether the work has been recognized as making a significant contribution to the field. Likewise, a not-so-significant project would not be accepted in a positive manner by colleagues, would not have received recognition, and perhaps was never published even though submitted to journals. Thus the respondents chose the research projects about which they were interviewed, and they used acceptance by other scholars in the discipline as the criterion for significance. We simply asked them to choose first the study for which they were most proud and for which they received the most recognition, and second, a study that they had completed but that generated little pride and that they might like to forget.

The next step was to develop a list of specific characteristics along which to compare the research projects. This involved two steps. The first step was a literature search for dimensions along which successful projects might be discriminated from nonsuccessful projects. This search included both the literature on research (Davis, 1971; Gottfredson, 1978), and the literature on organizational innovation that had used the method of comparing successful and unsuccessful projects (Zand and Sorensen, 1975; Science Policy Research Unit, 1972). We also did an informal survey of some of our colleagues, who were asked to provide their description of what characterized exceptionally poor research papers. From these sources a pool of 38 questionnaire items was developed that seemed to capture most characteristics by which significant and not-so-significant research might differ from one another. These 38 questions constitute the questionnaire used in this study. A copy of the questionnaire is included in Appendix D.

Semistructured Interviews. The open-ended responses from semistructured interviews with each investigator were designed to trace each project back to its beginning. General questions were asked, and then the interviewer continued to probe until he understood the history of the project. Example questions included: How did the project originate? Where did the idea come from? How was it developed? What attracted you to the project? What contextual factors facilitated or inhibited development of the research? Responses to these questions were written down by the interviewer. The open-ended questions are also listed in Appendix D.

Procedure. The face-to-face interviews were conducted first and lasted from 45 to 60 minutes. After completing the interviews each investigator was asked to use the questionnaire to describe both studies. Subjects were interviewed whenever was feasible, depending on the convergent travel schedules of interviewer and interviewee.

Caveat. After examination of the set of 29 written pairs of interviews, it became clear that the interview team (the three authors of this monograph) had not maintained rigorous consistency. In a few cases respondents chose projects that they especially liked or disliked, without regard for acceptance or rejection by the larger academic community. Interview technique, handwriting, abbreviations, follow-up probes, and perception of important points all differed by interviewer. On balance, however, the interviews yielded robust information. Most interviews pertained to research that was theoretical rather than methodological, and the designation of significance in most cases was compatible both with the judgment of the academic community and with the respondent's own taste. In sum we feel reasonably confident each subject understood the objectives of the study, that each interview probed the recollections of the subjects as thoroughly as possible, and that all relevant information was recorded, in some fashion or other.

RESULTS

OPEN-ENDED RESPONSES

Significant Research Projects

Excerpts from the open-ended interviews about the origin of significant research projects are in Figure 4.1. The paraphrases provide examples of the imagery associated with significant research projects as described by the respondents. Content analysis of the descriptions seem to indicate several antecedents to successful research.

(1) *Activity.* Significant research was an outcome of investigator activity and exposure. Frequent interactions, being in the right place at the right time, chance, and contact with management and with colleagues are related to the beginning of good research ideas. Investigator solitude and isolation proba-

FIGURE 4.1 Origins of Significant Research Projects

I threw out an idea in a doctoral seminar to which a student responded. Sense of great excitment, engagement in task, reading, thinking, interacting. Continuous interaction to test ideas against one another — couldn't let go. Original idea came from interaction with executives and learning the problems they faced.

Study evolved from 2-3 streams: libertarian view, visit with _____ who had similar ideas or conclusions, endless informal discussion, previous studies I had done, observation of people.

Wanted to develop theoretical rationale and interpretation for the seemingly confusing and contradictory empirical results concerning _____. Wanted to clarify and make sense of it, and colleagues agreed with importance.

Theoretically eloquent. Idea originated in a seminar where diverse backgrounds led to stimulating clashes. Connections plus enthusiasm.

Novel combination — new theoretical idea with interesting way to test it. Also did pilot study and boom, discovered a new factor that limited previous research.

Worked in _____, and personal experience contrasted with academic theory. Findings were politically relevant for understanding motivations of poor people.

We were playing bridge with a couple from marketing. He mentioned a problem, and I said that sounds like _____ theory. We got very excited. Solved an applied problem.

I was perplexed by some results, and at the same time I read a paper by someone else who had observed the same thing and was perplexed. Tested ideas to show that conventional wisdom was erroneous and provided much simpler strategy from prediction models.

I was the entrepreneur. I perceived the need and felt it was timely. I listened to clients and sensed their careers.

Real-world problems that could have policy implications. Also personal values — concern over Vietnam War. Came from real-life experience and reflection and not from literature.

The intent was to discover correct dimensions of the concept and clarify it for the literature. The concept was poorly conceptualized and was relevant to management.

FIGURE 4.1 Continued

Student had done an excellent paper. Decided spontaneously to collaborate with student, and was not an outgrowth of long-term interests.

The idea occurred as a result of studying literature relevant to this problem. Also playful, exploratory intellectual climate — lots of "what if" conversation.

Chance. It was a matter of being in a place that did this kind of work and having the right previous experience. Had both applied and theoretical implications.

Convergence of several things. Previous book, interest in this industry, interest in _____, wife's career, and ability to use new technique.

Grew from literature review, work over previous years, interaction with Ph.D. student, mathematical model developed previously, and the situation in which all this could be chunked.

From frustration over issues of motivation; from wondering how to motivate employees; from previous study of supervisors; from current literature.

A colleague walked in one day and tried to explain a new concept from operations research. Suddenly I realized significance for organizations. Multiple implications blossomed right in front of us. We talked for a year, were very excited, and finally wrote everything down.

It was a plight. I didn't believe in _____ and wanted to show it. I could use a high-powered methodology I had been taught. I meshed all my interests — small groups, personality, creativity, applied.

Dramatic topic and of interest to my associates. Methodology; was of long-standing interest to me. Current events influenced thinking, as did one or two key books.

---

bly would be less likely to result in significant research outcomes.

(2) *Convergence.* There is a sense that several activities or interests converge at the same time. This convergence might involve an idea with a method, or the interest of a colleague or student with exposure to an organizational problem or a new

technique. This is in some way related to the notion of activity because it is through activity and exposure that the investigator is able to be at the convergence of several streams.

(3) *Intuition*. The importance of the research and the interest in it seem to be guided by intuition and feeling rather than by logical analysis. Investigators often expressed a feeling of excitement or commitment, a perceived eloquence, as if they "knew" they were doing the right thing. A great deal of intrinsic interest is also present.

(4) *Theory*. A concern with theory also seems to be important. A primary goal often was to understand or explain something. The investigator was curious, was concerned with a puzzle, or wanted to clarify something that was poorly understood. Theoretical understanding of some aspect of organizations seems to be a primary goal of the research.

(5) *Real World*. Often the research problem had an applied, real-world flavor to it. They were not simply elaborations of abstract, academic ideas that were unrelated to organizations. The ideas often were tangible, useful, and pertained to ongoing organizational activities. Often the idea arose from contact with laypeople in organizations. Many significant investigations were about something real within organizations rather than about something imaginary as seen from outside of organizations.

Not-So-Significant Research

The paraphrases drawn from the discussion of not-so-significant research are in Figure 4.2, and they are characterized by quite different imaginary. The content of these responses suggests the following patterns.

(1) *Expedience*. A frequent theme is that the investigator undertook the research project because it was easy, cheap, quick, or convenient. A genuine contribution to knowledge apparently takes substantial thought and effort. Expedient short cuts tend to lead to insignificant outcomes.

FIGURE 4.2   Origins of Not-So-Significant Research

My heart was in other things. The research concerned demographic questions (age) and there was no reason or theory behind it.

Wanted to do a quick-and-dirty study for publication.

The topic was timely and new at the time and I thought I could mesh practical and theoretical issues. But the project was skewed to satisfy the funding agency, not me. A new car for me, but no theoretical contribution.

Low-grade interest in the project. Easy access to student population and had to show something for a year's sabbatical. Expedient. Mechanical giving of questionnaire. No novelty, no theory, no application to anyone. Have questionnaire, will travel.

Gathered data to try a statistical technique. I was fascinated by quantitative measurement techniques. It worked, but no theory.

The concept I tried to develop a measure for was of little use. I did not think through the conceptual foundations of the study very well.

Persuaded by a colleague to look at the question. Not theoretically motivated. Little attention to the process being studied.

Instrument development was shortchanged. Theoretical model was not well developed so the study became descriptive rather than model testing.

The theory was not complex enough — too mainstream, meat and potatoes. Data were just dull.

The data were cheap and easy to obtain. The idea came up because I was specifically thinking, "How can I get a publication out of this activity." Didn't think through problem or talk about it with colleagues.

Did it for money! Contract research. Nothing intrinisically interesting about the problem. Problem was nonexistent.

Colleagues wanted to do a joint paper for presentation at national meetings. Several sections of students were available so we distributed personality tests and questionnaires to them. Typology was not carefully developed.

Insufficient thought about research.

No real conceptual anchor or goals because there was no theory. Methods were adopted by anology. Let analysis do thinking.

(continued)

FIGURE 4.2 Continued

Convenient location. Proximity facilitated the study. Questionnaire was available from other research.

While doing dissertation, I discovered data base in government office. But the study dealt with minor modification of same old questions already in literature.

It was a replication of earlier project. Easy to do. Strictly mechanical. Reviewers recognized this, and it was never published. Method wasn't very good either.

I needed some research activity and a business student game was there to be used. Only reason for study was that it was "convenient."

(2) *Method*. Often a statistical technique or the method to be employed took priority over theory and understanding. The purpose of the study was simply to try out a methodological technique. In those cases the study may have been successfully completed and published, but the outcome was not very important.

(3) *Motivation*. The investigators were not motivated by a desire for knowledge and understanding of some organization phenomenon. They did the research because they wanted a possible publication, or money, or they were interested in other research projects. The absence of interest in the research problem or in the discovery of new knowledge tended to result in research that produced little new knowledge.

(4) *Lack of Theory*. Another common theme is that the investigator simply did not provide enough thought to make the study work. Complex theoretical issues had not been carefully worked through in advance. Theoretical development requires extensive intellectual effort. Without theory, the research may be easier and quicker, but the outcome will often be insignificant.

Summary

Interesting differences between significant and not-so-significant research have emerged from the open-ended interviews. An entirely different pattern of activities and motivations seem to distinguish significant from not-so-significant research. Significant research tends to be the result of broad exposure and activity, the convergence of several streams of thinking and ideas, an intuitive decision process, and a concern with theoretical understanding and with real-world problems. Not-so-significant research tends to result from expedience, from method replacing theory as the goal of the research, and from investigator motivation for such things as money or publication rather than new knowledge.

An alternative explanation is that self-report descriptions and attribution errors bias the statements about research antecedents. Respondents may ascribe successful outcomes to themselves and unsuccessful outcomes to external circumstances. This does not appear to be the case in the descriptions in Tables 4.1 and 4.2. Respondents indicated that internal motivations and personal decisions were generally the antecedents of not-so-significant research outcomes, thereby attributing failure to themselves. Significant research outcomes often resulted from interactions with colleagues and students, luck, and real-world activities.

CLOSED-ENDED RESPONSES

The closed-ended responses that seemed to discriminate between significant and not-so-significant research projects are listed in Table 4.1. These items are listed in rough order of the absolute score (on a five-point scale) combined with the difference from the score for not-so-significant projects. The themes

TABLE 4.1 Characteristics that Differentiate Successful from Not-So-Successful Research

Item	Score for Significant Research	Difference
To what extent would you say the methodology and argument were systematic, sound, rigorous, tight, and relatively error free? (31)*	4.3	1.7
To what extent did the project have implications that apply to the real world, such as being useful to managers or to teachers of introductory O.B. and I/O psychology courses (23)	3.7	1.5
To what extent did the project clarify a poorly understood or cloudy issue? (28)	3.9	1.3
To what extent would you say the methodology might be perceived as complex and sophisticated by the intended audience? (33)	4.0	1.2
To what extent would you say the primary reason for your research project reflected your personal interest and curiosity rather than acceptability and interest to the discipline? (11)	4.2	.8
To what extent were the variable of interest quantifiable in an objective rather than subject fashion (e.g., size easily quantifiable as counting number of employees; power is illusive and intangible)? (37)	4.0	.9
To what extent did the project help resolve a controversial or disputed issue in the literature? (27)	3.4	1.4
To what extent did you have firm expectations about the empirical outcomes? (30a)	3.6	1.0
To what extent would you say the primary reason for your research project was to apply a new research method or technique as a way to shed light on a well-established research problem? (1)	3.3	1.1
To what extent did the project apply to organization settings or individuals in general (rather than to limited type or to limited population within organizations)? (24)	3.4	.9
To what extent would you say the primary reason for your research project was to test directly competing theories or models about a phenomenon? (10)	3.0	1.2

TABLE 4.1 Continued

Item	Score for Significant Research	Difference
To what extent would you say the primary reason for your research project was to use an improved, more rigorous method than was previously used to study an established phenomenon (greater internal validity)? (4)	3.3	.9
To what extent did the project determine that diverse phenomena are united by a single explanation (simplification or integration)? (18)	2.9	1.2
To what extent did the project identify a relationship between variables that previously were believed not to be related? (15)	3.0	1.0

*Number in parenthesis keyed to questionnaire number (see Appendix D).

apparent from this table contain some overlap with the patterns in Tables 4.1 and 4.2 plus some additional ideas that were not covered in the open-ended discussions.

(1) *Rigor.* One frequent theme is that of intellectual and empirical rigor. Methodology and argument were systematic, sound, and relatively error free. Variables often were quantifiable and the methodology complex.

(2) *Importance to the Discipline.* Another theme seems to be the relevance to theoretical problems in the discipline. The research clarifies a poorly understood issue, helps resolve a controversial issue, tests directly competing theories, or may show that diverse phenomena are united by a single explanation. The outcome of the significant research thus makes a contribution to the theoretical knowledge base of the discipline.

(3) *Personal Interest and Motivation.* Significant research is more likely to be undertaken because of personal interests of the investigator rather than because the research is acceptable to the discipline (and publishable), and the investigator is likely to have beliefs about the expected outcome.

(4) *Real-World Implications.* The final theme concerns problems that are related to the real world, such as being useful

TABLE 4.2 Characteristics for Which Not-So-Significant Research Received a Higher Score than Significant Research

Item	Score for Not-So-Significant Research	Difference
To what extent would you say the primary reason for your research project was the opportunity to use a method that was convenient for you to execute (familiarity, expense, facilities, etc.)? (12)*	3.0	.6
To what extent would you say the primary reason for your research was the discovery or availability of a data base that enabled you to test ideas that were interesting to you? (13)	2.4	.3
To what extent would you say the primary reason for your research was to add a new variable or new combination of variables to the study of an established phenomena? (2)	2.3	.3

*Number in parentheses keyed to questionnaire numbers (see Appendix D).

to managers or to teachers. Significant research findings also apply to a wide range of organizational situations rather than to a very limited or narrowly defined population.

The significant research projects scored slightly higher or about the same than the not-so-significant projects on most other questionnaire items. For three questions, however, there was a reversal and the not-so-significant research received a higher score. Those three items are in Table 4.2. The differences are not large, but they are especially interesting because each of the items represented a legitimate reason for undertaking a research project.

(1) *Expedience.* Undertaking research because it was convenient or because of the availability of the data is more often a characteristic of not-so-significant research. This finding reflects a pattern similar to what we saw in the open-ended responses. Expedient and convenient research apparently does not lead to significant outcomes.

(2) *Lack of Theoretical Effort.* The third item in Table 4.2 pertains to the mechanical combination of variables rather than

to the effort to achieve theoretical understanding. Simply combining new variables to study a traditional phenomena will tend to be received with only modest interest.

DISCUSSION

The above findings must be treated as extremely tentative. They are based upon an exploratory study, a convenience sample, and subjective recollections of the research process. Despite the limitations of the study, some interesting and potentially useful patterns have emerged. At this point, we can once again raise the questions from the beginning of this chapter: What is the process by which scholars become engaged in significant organizational research? How can a researcher identify an innovative research project that will result in a substantial increment to knowledge? Based upon the findings described so far in this chapter, we can propose some tentative answers. These guidelines summarize the activities and processes that seem to lead to significant research outcomes.

GUIDELINES FOR SIGNIFICANT RESEARCH

(1) *Significant research is an outcome of investigator involvement in the physical and social world of organizations.* The implications for scholars is clear: Make contacts. Leave your office door open. Look for wide exposure and diverse experiences. Go into organizations. Discuss ideas with students and colleagues. Look for new methodologies. Listen to managers. Activity and exposure are important because significant research is often the chance convergence of ideas and activities from several sources. Investigators who remove themselves from these streams, who stay isolated, who do

research based upon the next logical step from a recent journal article, are less likely to achieve something outstanding.

(2) *Significant research is an outcome of investigator interest, resolve, and effort.* Significant research is not convenient. It is not designed to achieve a quick-and-dirty publication. It is not expedient. A great deal of effort and thought is required to transform difficult research problems into empirical results that are clear and useful. For most of us, there is no easy path. Genuine interest and great effort are needed to achieve significant outcomes.

(3) *Significant research projects are chosen on the basis of intuition.* When a project has the potential for high payoff, investigators "feel" good about it, they are excited, and that feeling seems to be an accurate indicator of future significance. The project is not chosen on the basis of logic or certainty of publication.

(4) *Significant research is an outcome of intellectual rigor.* Although the project may begin in a fuzzy state, it must end up well understood if it is to have impact. Substantial effort goes into theoretical development and clarification. The research method may be complex and sophisticated, which also requires careful thought and application. When a study turns out to be not so significant, it is often because the theory is not thought out. This may be the hardest part. Often a research technique can be applied quickly and easily, but without theoretical depth the study probably will not be outstanding.

(5) *Significant research reaches into the uncertain world of organizations and returns with something clear, tangible, and well understood.* Good research takes a problem that is not clear, is in dispute or out of focus, and brings it into resolution. Rigor and clear thinking are needed to make this transformation. Significant research begins with disorder, but ends with order. Successful research often reaches out and discovers order and understanding where none was perceived previously. The result is something specific and tangible that can be understood and used. Logic and certainty do not begin the process, but are an outcome of the process.

(6) *Significant research focuses on real problems.* Significant research does not simply build abstract concepts onto a purely academic structure. Significant research deals with the real world, and the findings have relevance for colleagues, teachers, or managers. Research that deals exclusively with the strains of artificial life created through scholarly inbreeding is less likely to be significant.

(7) *Significant research is concerned with theory, with a desire for understanding, and with explanation.* An important antecedent is curiosity and the excitement associated with understanding and discovery. Studies that are mechanical, that simply combine variables or use established data bases, seldom provide significant outcomes. When the primary motivation is publication, or money, or a research contract rather than theoretical understanding, then not-so-significant outcomes tend to emerge.

CONCLUSION

One important idea to emerge from this exploratory study of significant and not-so-significant research is that the selection of innovative research questions is not a single act or decision. Significant research is a process, an attitude, a way of thinking. Significant research is accomplished by people who are motivated to do significant research, who are willing to pay the cost in time and effort. Significant research is motivated by curiosity, by the desire to discover and understand. Investigators apparently are free to make the choices necessary to achieve significant outcomes. Among the people surveyed, most had been involved in both significant and not-so-significant research. Thus people can involve themselves in the types of activities conducive to significant research, and can select problems based upon their own interest and excitement. When they do, they are more likely to succeed.

Another important idea from this study is that significant research is characterized by a particular kind of *duality*. This notion goes beyond the data, but significant research seems to be characterized by both organic and mechanistic processes, by both linear and nonlinear thinking. Organic processes characterize the investigator's immediate world, and includes widespread contacts, involvement in many streams of research, and letting things happen that can converge and be exciting. The choice process for selecting research is often nonlinear, and is based on intrinsic interest and intuition. The research outcome, on the other hand, might be characterized as mechanistic. The successful project thus begins in an organic way, but ends up as a clearly defined, logical, rational product for diffusion to colleagues or managers. Perhaps this is why so much theoretical effort is required. Translating the poorly understood to the well understood requires intensity and commitment. It is a high-order activity. The research outcome defines some aspect of organizational reality for other people.

Organizational research is dull because it fails to capture the duality. Too much research starts with mechanistic, linear thinking, and ends up there as well. Investigators choose topics that are already well defined and make minor adjustments to them. Mechanistic processes dominate. Journal evaluations often are concerned with logic and rationality in both the beginning and ending of the project. By contrast, significant research often is characterized by uncertainty, fuzziness, and ambiguity in the initial stages. To achieve significant research, we must take a chance, we must make mistakes, we must probe beyond what we already know.

We hear much about scientific rigor, experimental control, measurement precision, and the anticipation and removal of uncertainties as the norm for good research. Our research training encourages us to get rid of anything that could upset the research blueprint, to be sure of what we are doing, to define the problem precisely. The shortcoming of a mechanistic beginning is that it assumes investigators know a substantial amount about the phenomenon under investigation. Knowledge beforehand makes for clean, tidy research, but the significance will typically be small. If we know in advance what the research answer will be, if we understand the phenomenon well enough to predict and control what happens, then we have not chosen an appropriate problem. We have not probed into the organizational milieu to learn something new. If we are to acquire genuinely new knowledge, then we will not know the answer in advance. We will not even be sure that there is an answer. The significant discoveries, the good science, require us to go beyond the safe certainty of mechanistic research projects.

The notion that we must begin with uncertainty, even build uncertainty into our research, may be the key. It is important to ask research questions without having the answer in advance. The only requirement is that we end up with some level of certainty. In one sense, then, scientific progress requires both the organic and mechanistic. We must begin with the organic nad finish with the mechanistic. To some extent we must bring organic processes into our research lives in order to be exposed to the exciting, unanticipated convergence of ideas that has the potential to be outstanding. If our research starts out neat and tidy and mechanistic, and the results come out as expected, then it was probably a waste of time.

AN ADDENDUM: SOME RESEARCH MILESTONES

As a fun thing to do, one of the authors made a short list of what might be considered research milestones in the study of organizational behavior and then called the people responsible and asked them how the idea for the study (or studies) came to be. A "milestone" was a research study (or series of studies) thought to be especially important because of the new direction it gave to the field, the specific problems it solved, or the amount of subsequent research it stimulated. Whether or not its conceptual foundation was necessarily "correct" was not the principal concern. We do not mean to pretend that this is any kind of ultimate list. It is merely our own opinion and we did not spend much time generating it. Other people may have generated a different.

The basic procedure was simply to identify the principal investigator and then call him or her on the telephone. If there was more than one choice for who to designate as principal investigator, we opted for whomever was easiest to contact. The telephone interviews followed the same general protocol as the "within-investigators" study described in the first part of this chapter. That is, we asked the principal investigator to recall how the research question(s) that generated the milestone was developed, who had the original idea, how it was modified, the context in which it occurred, and so forth. Everyone cooperated to the best of their recollection and it was an enjoyable, though brief, experience for the experimenter.

The list of milestones and principal investigators is shown in Figure 4.3. So as not to create awkward moments at the Methods Conference we omitted people from the Planning Committee, even though they might have created a good many milestones in their day. We also omitted people who has already been included in the "within-investigator" sample. Thus there is no overlap between this sample and the previous one.

SOME INFERENCES

Based on the telephone interviews with the people listed in Figure 4.3, the following general conclusions seemed reasonable.

(1) Milestones are not generated by testing propositions from someone else's "theory," by seeing if moderator X works for relationship Y, and so on. The investigator must develop a tool or treatment that will have wide implications for important problems, or must do a lot of research that culminates

Douglas Bray	The AT&T Management Progress Study and the development of the assessment center
Fred Fielder	The research studies upon which the Contingency Model of leadership is based
Ed Fleishman	The development of the Ohio State leader behavior measures
Ed Fleishman	The studies dealing with the interaction of learning and the structure of psychomotor abilities
J.R.P. French	The Coch and French study of participation in decision making at Harwood
Robert Ford	The initial AT&T studies on the effects of job enrichment
Frederick Herzberg	The initial study of engineers and accountants that led to the "two-factor theory"
Ernest McCormick	The research that led to the development of the Position Analysis Questionnaire (PAQ)
Edwin Locke	The initial series of studies on the effects of goal setting on performance
Frank Schmidt	The development and test of the generalizability model of test validities
Melvin Sorcher	The development of the social interaction modeling training strategy
Patricia Cain Smith	The development of the Job Descriptive Index
Patricia Cain Smith	The development of behavior expectation scaling

FIGURE 4.3   A List of I/O Research Milestones

in a new direction or new "truth" that is fundamentally important for redirecting the efforts of researchers or practitioners.

(2) In almost every single case the substantive theory or knowledge for generating the milestone did not come from within the field. It was brought in from outside because the field was found narrow, sterile, and wanting. Well over half the principal investigators expressed considerable frustration over the inability of the literature to provide help.

(3) In almost every case the force driving the effort was a specific and important problem to be solved. It was not a method or technique (independent variable) in search of a problem (dependent variable) to solve. It was very definitely the other way around. Thus, for this particular sample of individuals,

there is a higher correspondence with research needs as expressed by people in organizations (Chapter 3) than by the published literature (Chapter 1).

(4) In every case the principal investigators were deeply immersed in the substantive content of the problem at issue and did an awfully lot of work. Milestones do not come easy.

(5) On the surface, for most of the milestones, the creation or development of the research problem appeared to have an element of luck, as it sometimes did for the previous sample of investigators. However, in these instances it was *not* a case of fortuitous happenstance or being in the right place at the right time. All these efforts were in the mainstream of the individual's concern and were in a very real sense "made to happen" because the individual was (and is) smart, knowledgeable, and inquisitive. As they say in sports, you must make your own breaks. They will not just happen.

COMMENT

The results of these interviews were quite consistent with the information collected from the previous sample of investigators. The overall impression is one of very hard working people who were deeply immersed in the work they were doing but who were not isolated within one domain of literature or within the four walls of their office. They were engrossed in a problem that was in direct line with their interests and they were able to exploit innovative solutions from other domains when they saw them.

5

Toward More Satisfying Research Questions

☐ This is the really uncomfortable part. Up to this point we have tried to stay reasonably close to the information we collected and not stray too far into out-and-out pontification. We have now run out of data and it is time to say what we can about how our problem finding and question development might be enhanced. Such enhancement could come about in two major ways, either by prescribing things that people should do with greater frequency or by proscribing things that researchers should not do. This chapter will attempt to summarize a number of possible strategies within each of these two major categories.

At this point we also should be reminded of several obvious truths. First, no set of rules or strategies will guarantee that any of us will discover interesting research problems, develop effective research questions, and/or reap the benefits of highly acclaimed research productivity. We can only hope that these strategies can somehow increase the probability of doing research of which the investigator will be proud.

Second, the criteria for what is good research are not absolutes. To a significant extent they are a function of the value system within which the investigator operates and the particular point in time at which the research takes place. Consequently, we cannot look at a specific research question and say with finality that it is a good or bad one. At some time and under some set of circumstances such a judgment may have to be revised. However, it also seems true that some research questions are so obviously valuable that it is difficult to think of circumstances under which they would not be viewed positively. Similarly, some research questions seem beyond redemption.

Finally, we are acutely aware that there are no special reasons for anointing the three of us to make the statements in this chapter. Many others could have done it better.

The material for this final chapter was generated in several ways. The pieces of information gathered for the previous chapters and the generalizations they suggested were a major source, and we have attempted to summarize this material in some coherent fashion. We also surveyed the literature to see if anyone else had spoken to these same issues and whether their pontifications agree with ours. Since we are trying to deal with innovation, the literature on creative problem solving was also examined. Finally, the workshop participants reacted to all this material and offered their own opinions. We hope we have done justice to their ideas.

What should current and prospective researchers do? First, we would like to focus on the positive side and consider proactive behaviors that might enhance problem finding and question generation. Within that category the subtopics will consist of strategies for developing new knowledge, generating wider experience, breaking established sets, applying creative strategies, and having ideas confronted. The negative side will consist of a list of don'ts. In effect, such a list constitutes a checklist against which investigators can evaluate their problem-finding behavior and the research questions it generates. If very many items on the checklist receive a negative score, then the advice is to change direction. Finally, we will talk a bit about the "publish-or-perish contingency," as is is too frequently implemented, and about what effects it seems to have on research in our field.

STRATEGIES TO ENHANCE THE DEVELOPMENT OF MORE SATISFYING RESEARCH QUESTIONS

The term "satisfying" is used here to reinforce the notion that whether a research question is good or bad is at least in part an idiographic judgment and cannot be completely normative in nature. Thus, if in the face of whatever list of dos and don'ts is presented, an investigator insists that a particular question is an interesting one, we cannot argue.

DEVELOPING NEW KNOWLEDGE

If the interviews reported in Chapter 4 said anything, it was that satisfying research questions flow from a thorough knowledge of the topic. There really is no substitute for a total immersion in state-of-the-art knowledge. It also seems apparent, from the interviews with investigators and from our own experience, that this kind of knowledge and expertise does not come from a general reading and studying of the literature, no matter how much time is spent doing that. To become *really* familiar with a topic the effort must be focused in some way such that the investigator is virtually forced to demonstrate his or her understanding publicly. That is, it is a long way from thinking you understand something to demonstrating your expertise to other people in some public fashion.

Some alternative methods for requiring yourself to achieve such a state of immersion are the following.

- *Teaching a course.* Preparing to teach a course for the first time is almost always a humbling experience. Gaps in knowledge become apparent, sterile concepts must be admitted to, and wishful thinking must be separated from data-based conclusions. If the course is at an advanced level and it is the investigator's primary responsibility to organize and present the material, then it can frequently serve the purpose of providing the kind of knowledge base we are talking about here.

- *Writing a review paper.* Whatever the motivation (naiveté, intimidation, money), one may attempt to write a critical review of some body of literature. It may be for a refereed journal, a convention presentation, a conference paper, or any other such forum. If the prospective audience is perceived to be a sophisticated one, generating the paper should force one into a careful consideration of what that particular body of literature is all about.

- *Writing proposals.* It is frequently the case that we write proposals for research because an employer or sponsor requested it or because a particular funding agency is interested in a particular question. As suggested by the results of the study reported in Chapter 4, this is not the way satisfying research studies are generated. However, the act of generating the proposal may provide a better knowledge base from which to generate more useful research questions, *if* the topic is one that interests you. Consequently, the effort put into developing the proposal may have long-term payoffs even if the original research question was not a particularly useful one.

- *Taking responsibility for special projects.* There are a variety of other tasks that applied behavioral scientists might engage in that would serve these same purposes. Preparing position papers for one's professional association, serving as a consultant on the preparartion of legislation, and creating planning documents for your employer are only a few examples. The principal requirement is that the projects require the individual to delve into the existing knowledge at some length and at the state-of-the-art level.

The purpose of listing the above possibilities is not to advocate being constantly "busy" with all of them. You could drown in a sea of your own expertise. However, we do believe that you must engage in some of these activities some of the time. Without it, you may never develop the kind of intense familiarity with a topic that you need so as to recognize a useful research question when you see one.

GENERATING A WIDER VARIETY OF EXPERIENCE

The literature on creative problem solving (e.g., Stein, 1974) *strongly* suggests that innovation typically does *not* come from an intense scrutiny of one's own field. Rather, it tends to be generated by exposing oneself to a variety of other people and ideas. This notion was strongly confirmed by the interviews we did with established investigators, which were reported in Chapter 4. This was one of the strongest themes that differentiated research questions investigators were proud of from research problems they would rather forget. It was also highly characteristic of the origins of the research milestones listed in the addendum to Chapter 4. You simply cannot sit in your office and ponder the research and practice in your own field day after day, month after month.

What are some strategies for generating these wider experiences and increasing the probability that new ideas might be discovered? At the risk of belaboring the obvious, we list the following.

- *Attending conventions and conferences.* All cynical and derisive laughter aside, spending a certain amount of time at conventions and conferences is more advantageous than spending all that time locked away in your office. It does give you an opportunity to talk with a variety of other people and to test your ideas against theirs. Further, all your available convention time should not be spent listening and talking with people just like you. If you define your "interests" rather narrowly and then spend all your time attending sessions and talking with people who share your interests, you are violating this strategy. People in other disciplines or subfields frequently approach many of the same issues in a very different form. Seek them out.

- *Increase interdisciplinary contact.* Most of us probably work within the context of a larger organization. Within most such organizations there are people in other fields worrying about the same kinds of issues, but from different perspectives. We should not pass up opportunities to interact with such people. Such opportunities should be created. If your organization does not provide such contacts, then you must go outside. Even various kinds of social events have been known to produce innovative research problems.

- *Contacts with the "real" world.* Many interesting and innovative research problems have been stimulated by conversations with real people who talk about their problems at work. Every student of organizations should do a considerable amount of this kind of informal interviewing. A useful exercise is then to translate the issues that come up in such conversations into researchable questions. Continual practice on this exercise would make the process almost automatic and the probability of missing *the* question, should it choose to stare you in the face, would be minimized.

- *The exploratory case study.* The above process can be formalized by turning it into a more systematic case study. That is, given that you have an interest in a certain area of organizational life and some tentative research questions in mind, pick out a few people who work in that area and interview them. Ask them a lot of questions about what they do, what problems they have, what changes they would like to see, what they would like to see preserved, what advice they would give to people just entering a job like theirs, and so on. For once, do not be so structured and purposive. Just be thorough. The objectives of this kind of case study are to refine the research questions to be studied later and to identify the parameters and conditions that might change the interpretation of the result.

- *Introspection.* Most of us work in organizations. We have a job. We have satisfactions and dissatisfactions. Our performance is assessed by some means or other. We operate within a network of motivational contingencies. In short, it is quite legitimate to search our own minds for ideas, so long as we play the role of job holder and not that of a detached observer. Be your own first subject. It might lead to something.

The same caveat is in order for this set of strategies as for the previous ones. All your time cannot be spent acquiring wider experiences. In addition, without a firm grasp of your own discipline, a wider set of experiences most likely will not pay back any dividends. The investigators in our interview sample were able to recognize new ideas when they saw them because they were very knowledgeable people. The recommendation to "get out of your office" a significant proportion of the time is not a license to avoid the intense study of your own field.

BREAKING ESTABLISHED SETS

Both the literature on creativity (e.g., Stein, 1974, 1975) and our everyday experience suggests that our problem-solving behavior sometimes gets into ruts, or standard ways of looking at things, from which it is difficult to extract ourselves. Research questions keep taking the same form, the same topics keep being researched, and a small number of methods and procedures are used over and over again. The major reason for having the conference on which these six volumes are based was to develop new strategies and methods for breaking out of our research ruts. The fact that the conference received the support that it did provides some evidence that this point of view is rather widely shared by people in the field.

Suggestions for breaking out of the established patterns can take at least two forms. First, we could offer actual substantive suggestions for what research questions are *really* the most important and which should be pursued in the years ahead. Second, we could search for strategies or heuristics that might have general applicability for getting us out of conventional patterns and into new ones.

We would like to discuss both of these in turn, beginning with some general strategies or processes that one might implement. Some of these come from the literature on creativity and the formal attempt to use science to develop methods for promoting innovation. Others are a bit more seat of the pants and are included here because they sound good or because we think we have seen them work.

STRATEGIES FROM THE LITERATURE ON CREATIVITY

It may seem a bit paradoxical to talk about rules to enhance creativity, since creativity is seen by many as an unstructured, intuitive process that transcends rules and order. Nevertheless, the enhancement of creativity and innovation in complex problem solving has been an intriguing issue for many years for scientist and nonscientist alike, and a certain amount of literature has been generated on the topic (e.g., Stein, 1975). Perhaps it is no accident that the site for the Innovations in Methodology Conference was the Center for Creative Leadership, an organization that conducts research on creativity and that offers an extensive series of programs in training for innovation (CCL, 1982).

It is not our intent to review the literature on creativity in detail or to discuss strategies for creativity enhancement at any length. We wish only to outline some suggestions and identify some additional reading that might be relevant for research problem finding and question development.

Unfortunately, some of the creativity enhancement strategies are most useful in group settings and cannot be implemented by a single individual. However, one benefit of a group technique is that it provides the investigator with a good excuse for interacting with his or her colleagues in a structured and mutually beneficial way. It might even be better than going to lunch at the same old place.

Brainstorming

Most readers are probably familiar with the rules of the brainstorming technique and the history of its origins in the world of advertising (Osborn, 1963). It is a widely used practice. For example, it was part of the original procedure developed at AT&T for getting suggestions from supervisors as to how jobs should be redesigned (Ford, 1969). That is, supervisors of the job in question were asked to brainstorm ideas for how the job should be changed. There is a certain amount of research that supports the conclusion that brainstorming groups produce higher quality, or more creative, ideas than conventional, garden-variety problem-solving groups (Meadow & Parnes, 1959).

Why not use brainstorming to "discover" the real issues in a topic, articulate specific questions, suggest alternative methods, or speculate about the consequences of studying something a certain way. All that is needed are a small number of colleagues that are willing and able. We realize that people frequently already do something like this in an informal way. However, we would bet that the rules of brainstorming (e.g., *no* criticism of others' ideas) are not followed very closely for very long. It might be worth at least one good faith attempt to take turns brainstorming each other's research-related problems. The group members would have a greater chance of learning different perspectives and perhaps more innovative ideas.

Some of the issues that might be brainstormed under the label of problem finding and question development are the following.

- What are the real issues in a particular domain of organizational life (e.g., the recruitment of scientific and engineering personnel during the next ten years, training skilled employees as the public school system continues to teach less and less)?
- What specific research questions flow from interest in a particular issue or topic?
- What are some alternative ways of asking a specific research question?

The rules of brainstorming are not hard to master. All that is really needed is the time and a small number of colleagues who are willing to experiment with you.

The Nominal Group Technique

Another group strategy is the nominal group technique (NGT). It differs from brainstorming in that group members present ideas in serial order and keep going around the group until everyone's fund of ideas is exhausted. During idea generation no one can say *anything* about someone else's idea, except to suggest elaborations or different variations when their turn comes. Thus at this stage there is no group interaction. Only after all ideas are generated can each idea then be evaluated and discussed; however, this must be done for each idea in turn. It is a long but very thorough process.

A good source book for both brainstorming and the nominal group technique is provided by Del Becq, Van de Ven, and Gustafson (1975). These authors also summarize some of the research pertaining to both methods.

The principal reasons for the development of the nominal group technique was to overcome the negative effects of face-to-face interactions on the quantity and quality of group problem solving (Maier, 1967). That is, it has been repeatedly demonstrated that the conventional, garden-variety problem-solving group, as can be found in virtually any organization, falls short of using all the knowledge its individual members have to offer. One of the contributors to this "shortfall" seems to be face-to-face interaction that permits all kinds of interpersonal behavior to compete with problem solving behavior. Brainstorming tries to overcome the shortfall by keeping the group focused on idea generation, which many would argue is the most neglected step in problem solving, and by not permitting criticism or evaluation of ideas. The nominal group technique simply forbids group interaction until all possible alternative ideas have been generated.

One tidbit of information that might interest the reader is that the nominal group technique was used by the Methods Conference planning committee as part of their procedure for generating possible workshop topics. That is, the idea for a workshop presentation devoted to problem finding and research question generation was generated in the course of using NGT.

The Delphi Technique

A procedure that goes even further than the nominal group technique and eliminates face-to-face interaction entirely is the Delphi procedure (Del Becq et al., 1975). While it was not really designed for idea generation there is no reason why the technique could not be used for this purpose. In brief, the procedure is as follows. The issue, question, or problem is presented to each group member individually, usually in writing. Each individual then generates an independent response. Thus there is really no need for the group member to be in the same room, the same building, or even in the same city. Individual responses are then collated, copies are made, and everyone's response is shown to everyone else. No editorial changes are made by any outside party at this point. After reviewing everyone else's initial response, each individual submits a revised response and the cycle is repeated. Ideally, the procedure would go through enough cycles to achieve some kind of convergence. The Delphi technique was originally developed to deal with problems like forecasting population trends, deaths from nuclear exchanges, and sales trends. With such problems convergence is usually achieved after two or three cycles.

If the Delphi were to be used in our context it might be applied to problems like:

- What is the most important research issue in a particular topic area (e.g., improvement of the quality of working life), and why?

- What are the three most important specific research questions that should be asked as regards a particular research issue (e.g., How should the quality of working life be assessed?)?

- What are three alternative ways of asking a particular research question, and what are the pros and cons for each alternative?

One major advantage of this procedure is that the first cycle virtually forces everyone to provide their best independent contribution and to describe it thoroughly enough for it to stand alone as a written document. Group members cannot remain silent. They can hide their lack of ideas with humor or bluster. They cannot reveal only that tidbit they know best. The technique also forces individuals to make the best use they can of the information provided by the other group members. Consequently, the chances of losing relevant information and ideas are minimized. A major disadvantage is the sheer amount of work involved. If the individual written responses are at all lengthy, the amount of effort required of each person is considerable.

These advantages and disadvantages were illustrated quite nicely when one of the authors (the oldest one) used the Delphi procedure to help a committee write a research proposal. Using committees to generate written products is a thankless task under any circumstances. It is especially difficult when there are time constraints and innovation is required. The six people on the committee were *each* asked to write a draft of a complete proposal. All six versions were then shown to all committee members and each person was asked to revise their own proposal and resubmit it. It was a painful experience and a lot of work but the resulting final draft was a very workable document and it did not look like it was written by a committee. After just these two cycles there was little difficulty in agreeing upon what the final draft should include. When one considers the endless "meetings" it may have taken to do this task in the usual way, the Delphi procedure may not have been all that much more expensive in terms of individual time commitment. However, it is probably much less work spending twenty hours in committee meetings than it is in spending twenty hours putting something down on paper. Most people probably prefer to sit and talk than to sit and write.

In sum, in spite of its costs, we believe the Delphi procedure does have much to recommend it when a group is faced with the task of developing innovative research questions. Small groups of colleagues might seriously consider investing time in it.

Methods to Enhance Productive and Divergent Thinking by Individuals

The literature on creativity encompasses a fairly large number of methods designed to facilitate the generation of new and/or novel ideas by individuals. Summaries are provided by Schaude (1979) and Stein (1974). For the most part there is not a large body of empirical research that supports, or does not support, any specific method. A small number of systematic studies do exist, but the bulk of the support for most of these techniques is provided by case studies (e.g., a previously intractable problem was solved by using this method) and by the perceived positiveness of the practitioner's experiences with them.

Our purpose here is not to review the evaluation literature on creativity enhancement techniques. Rather, we would simply like to summarize some of the principal methods that might be used if the reader was interested. Data are not available to argue either that they are a waste of time or that they will significantly enhance the probability of discovering interesting and satisfying research questions.

Synectics. This is one of the most well known methods designed to enhance divergent individual idea generation, but as marketed by Synectics, Inc., it does require the services of an expert leader (Prince, 1970). The method proceeds by taking a specific "problem as given" as a starting point. The problems used as examples in the synectics literature are almost always engineering or technical problems of one kind or another. The problem solver is then asked to restate problems in terms that he or she understands best and to cast out (purge) all solutions previously shown to be unworkable. With the help of the expert, the problem solver then proceeds to identify the problem, as restated, with a number of different kinds of analogies and then tries to generate as many implications of the analogy as possible.

For example, if you wanted to explore the problem of what research questions to ask about job stress one might think of a fish under stress. The fish might be under stress because of the water pressure at great depths, the lack of light, and the abundance of predators. How do various fish cope in this situation? Do these methods have analogies in the organization? What happens when the coping methods fail? What organizational research questions does this suggest? This kind of analogy is called the *direct* analogy. That is, something in nature is made directly analogous to the problem at issue. With the synectics technique direct analogies are usually mechanical or biological in nature.

Another type of analogy is the *personal* analogy in which you imagine yourself as the problem. For example, you might think of yourself as being under great stress from all sides. What information do you really want and think would help you in this situation? For example, just to pursue this analogy a bit, you might want to know how long the stress will last. If it is long term you will act differently than if it is short term. Now, although the present authors are not intimately familiar with current research on organizational stress, we do not believe that the duration question has really been given much attention. If five minutes of reasoning by personal analogy will produce one such question, think what hours and hours would do — perhaps. The books by Gordon (1961) and Prince (1970) are a place to start. The more seriously inclined could take the basic course offered by Synectics, Inc.

Creative Confrontation. As outlined by Schaude (1979), there are a number of strategies designed to juxtapose the problems at issue against some set of unrelated ideas and then require the problem solver to try to make connections between them and to identify possible implications. In the course of doing this, the problem solver may hit upon solutions that might not have been considered otherwise. For example, with the method of *stimulus* analysis the problem of how to improve the quality of working life might be juxtaposed against the following stimuli.

Club Med	Big league baseball
Fine wine	Hybrid seed corn

Now, what are the characteristics of fine wine that have implications for increasing the quality of working life. If fine wine is aged for a long time in the bottle, what does that imply about jobs? Should we promote more stability and longer tenure? A number of implications from each of the stimuli should be pursued.

Another variation of the same method would be to use unrelated pictures instead of written phrases. Still another variation, called *semantic intuition,* requires the problem solver to make up new words or phrases by selecting from unrelated lists of simpler words and then brainstorming the possible implications of the new set of phrases for the problem at hand.

Systematic Restructuring. Another set of methods has to do with breaking down the given problem into as many subparts as possible and then looking for structure among the parts. For example, into how many different subproblems can the problem of enhancing the quality of working life be broken? Are there some common themes among the subparts?

A COMMENT ON INDIVIDUAL CREATIVITY METHODS

We are not advocating that every reader spend one hour or two hours a day exercising his or her divergent thinking skills. The above examples of creativity enhancement methods are included only to illustrate that there is a relatively large literature on this topic, a number of specific methods do exist, they have been put into practice, they are generating at least some research, and there are a number of serious-minded people who think they have value. Whether at this point they have significant utility for students of organizations searching for more useful research questions we do not know.

However, one of the methods is especially intriguing and has to do with the exercise of using personal analogy. It fits with our conviction that we do not use ourselves as subjects often enough. Over the years we have been continually surprised at the number of investigators who do not pretest their research questions, assessment techniques, or experimental procedures on themselves, and then examine their own reactions in detail. For example, if one is interested in the construct of job commitment, imagine yourself as possessing a high or low level of commitment in a specific situation. What is it that you want people to know about how you feel? Is commitment really the best way to describe it? Can a questionnaire that uses very general and very brief items capture the way you feel? If an investigator went through this exercise for a number of different levels of commitment in several possible job situations, we believe that the subsequent formulation of the research question would be both different and more useful.

Our second choice for which method might have most value would be the exercise of decomposing a research problem into as many specific components or subquestions as possible. Even though the question that is eventually researched may represent a common theme among a number of components, we believe that much question asking in our field is at such a general level that the answers that are obtained are not all that useful. For example, does job satisfaction correlate with age? Is management development effective? How should individual performance be assessed? Each of these can be broken down into a number of specific subquestions, at least some of which would be far more useful than the general question? We think it would be a useful exercise to push this to the extreme so as to find out which components represent the orthogonal parts and which do not.

Finally, we think the group methods are especially valuable. They do provide ways for groups of colleagues to get together and systematically consider problems that interest them. Although success cannot be guaranteed, we think a certain amount of time devoted to this procedure would be of considerable value.

THE CONVENTIONAL WISDOM AND ITS CONVERSE

The creativity literature deals with strategies that are meant to be generally applicable to a wide range of problem-solving situations. There are many other heuristics for generating research problems that have a more specific form. For example, McGuire (1979) lists 45 of them for consideration by social psychologists. We would like to take up one of them in some detail because it seems particularly applicable to our situation.

Every discipline has its conventional wisdoms. Some may be true and some may be false. Some may be very valuable and some may be harmful. We do not wish to argue the relative goodness or badness of any particular conventional wisdoms. Instead, our suggestion is that every student of organizations spend at least some time at the following exercise.

(1) List as many of the conventional wisdoms in your field as you can.

(2) State the converse of each conventional wisdom.

(3) Consider the kinds of research questions that are suggested by assuming the converse to be true, even if they may not seem reasonable at first. Pursue this kind of question asking until you have assured yourself that you have explored the major implications of assuming the converse. Do any of the questions genuinely intrigue you? Discuss the list with your colleagues.

This exercise is very much in line with the conclusions reached by Davis (1971), who argued that the most interesting research questions are those that deny at least some assumptions long thought to be true. While there is no guarantee that the questions suggested by the converse of a conventional wisdom will be useful ones, our collective experience and the literature reviewed by Davis says that it happens often enough to make the exercise worthwhile.

For what they are worth, we offer our own list of conventional wisdoms in Figure 5.1.

Just to take one example from this list, suppose we adopt the position that job stress is good, not bad. What research questions might this suggest? Consider the following.

• Is the reaction referred to as stress multidimensional? Are some reactions evaluated positively and some negatively?

FIGURE 5.1   Some Conventional Wisdoms and their Converses

Conventional Wisdom	*Converse*
(1) Objective "hard" criteria are best. They are the most reliable and the most directly tied to the organization's goals. They are the most important in the overall scheme of things	Objective criteria are the worst. They lack construct validity, are biased, and are really only subjective measures at least one step removed. Deal with subjectivity up front. We will learn more.
(2) Large bureaucratic organizations are bad for the people who work in them. They stifle innovation, reward conformity, and do not care about individuals.	Large bureaucratic organizations are good. For example, they provide a stability and consistent level of rewards not matched elsewhere.
(3) Job stress is bad. It leads to dysfunctional behaviors.	Job stress is good. It makes jobs more stimulating and interesting.
(4) Organizations change people.	People change organizations.
(5) Individual productivity is declining in the United States.	Individual productivity is not declining and may be increasing.
(6) We need to know the ability requirements of jobs.	We do not need to know the ability requirements of jobs.
(7) We need both a "micro" and "macro" approach to understanding organizational behavior.	No we do not. It is a false dichotomy. We simply want to find the most direct antecedent that we can.
(8) Multivariate analyses are better than univariate analyses	Multivariate analyses are almost always misused. It would be better to change the research question to fit a univariate model.
(9) Our ability to predict job performance is very poor.	Our predictive validities are really quite good.
(10) In general, training has little (demonstrated) effect.	Training has very important effects on job behavior.
(11) We should try to increase the quality of working life	We should try to decrease the quality of working life.
(12) We should study the regularities and consistencies in behavior.	We should study inconsistencies, unstable, and/or abrupt changes in behavior.

- Is "stress" evaluated positively or negatively depending on how it is scheduled (e.g., periods of long duration versus short duration)?

- Do some "stressors" produce negative reactions and some positive?

- Does the same stressor affect some people positively and others negatively?

- Are the effects of a stressor determined almost entirely by the context in which it occurs?

- What stressors should we purposely build into a job?

Again, we do not mean to imply that either the conventional wisdom or its converse is more true, but only that considering the converse may lead to research questions that investigators might not otherwise have considered.

There are also a number of other such heuristics that can be used. For example, a useful exercise at some stage might be to restate your favorite research question in as many different forms as you can, or identify all the hidden value judgments that you can (e.g., performance is our most important dependent variable) and then take the opposing view to see what it implies about how research questions should be asked differently.

The optimal set of heuristics for finding and developing research problems is not yet known and readers are encouraged to explore their own. We now turn from the divergent to the convergent.

THINGS TO AVOID

This section is more negativistic in tone than the last one. It is a list of things to avoid if one's goal is to formulate specific research questions about substantive issues that are useful for the field, satisfying to the investigator, and positively evaluated by peers. The items on the list come from the opinions of the current authors, the opinions of the investigators we interviewed, the opinions of the sample we surveyed, the "literature" on such opinions (e.g., Barrett, 1972; Bass, 1974; Dunnette, 1965, 1974), and the opinions of the participants in the workshops presented at the Innovations in Methodology Conference in Greensboro. We hope this is not more opinion than the reader can tolerate.

In effect, the items on the list are intended to be a checklist against which an investigator can compare a particular research problem or question. Unfortunately, we have no scoring system developed via thorough criterion-referenced methods that will indicate when to proceed because all is well, when to move ahead with caution, when to fall back and reformulate, and when to drop everything and run for your professional life. In no particular order, the list is as follows.

(1) Unless the concern is specifically with research on analytic methods themselves, do not choose the method before the question. If you find yourself saying things like, "Now that I have mastered path analysis what can I apply it to?" or "Canonical correlation is great, where can I find some data on which to use it?" *stop* immediately and rethink your priorities. Too often we become enthralled with the beauty of particular analytic methods and they become ends in themselves. It detracts from thinking about the real issue, which is the substantive question that must be answered.

(2) Related to the above is the tendency to get too embroiled in the computerization of data analysis. Computers are becoming ever more seductive and many of our respondents commented that some investigators they knew (not themselves certainly) frequently seemed to change the nature of their project to make it more appropriate for computer analysis. This will become more and more of a problem for topic areas such as technical skills training, in which the potential for a completely automated training center is not far away. However, computer sophistication, no matter how advanced, cannot make up for inadequate instructional objectives, inadequate instructional content, and inadequate attention to instructional and learning principles. Computer hardware, computer software, analytic methods, and the like are not the highest priority. That place

must be reserved for the formulation of the substantive question itself. If you find yourself turning into a computer worshiper, stop and seek the appropriate kind of counseling.

(3) Do not try to "capture" the publication policies of journals and journal editors and conduct research that you think will conform to those policies. In the view of our respondents, this does not work very well and leads to very pedestrian investigation. It is also true that most journal editors think their so-called gate-keeping function is almost completely constrained by the nature of the manuscripts that come in the door and they would like nothing better than to violate the policies that people think they use. If investigators spend too much time trying to "psych out" the publication system, it may mean they have no real substantive interests of their own and they should be in a different line of work.

(4) If you find yourself attempting to "test" a "model" of organizational behavior consisting of several boxes connected by arrows, by writing self-report questionnaire items to "measure" each major variable in the model, stop. This particular paradigm has not proven very useful and its ultimate accomplishment will be a theory of questionnaire behavior, not organizational behavior. Almost everyone we interviewed or surveyed warned of this danger. Some were quite vocal about it.

(5) Be wary of posing a research question that cannot be answered. In general, questions of the form, "Does A or B account for more variance in C?" fall in this category. The answer may be completely determined by the relative variance in A and B, which in turn may be a function of a large number of other things. Whether ability or motivation is more important in determining performance, the relative influence of job commitment and job stress on job satisfaction, and the relative influence of the leader versus the informal work group are all examples of this kind of question. Covered up by each of these comparisons are a number of more useful questions that should be asked instead. For example, what are some alternative ways that supervisors and the informal work group can provide a

specific kind of job outcome? Other questions of this type are: Does management training work? Can the XYZ model of leadership be supported? or other general questions for which a general answer provides very little information.

(6) Avoid asking questions to which we already know the answer. Making this determination can best be handled by asking a variety of colleagues to be candid, at a very early stage in the proceedings.

(7) Try not to investigate certain problems merely because they are feasible ones to investigate, as when there is a ready sample available, or even when there are funds available. If you do not have a genuine interest and curiosity in the problem, the study probably will not amount to very much.

(8) Unless you have a strong intrinsic interest in a specific question that has one of these forms, try not to plan studies that search for "moderators" of some previously investigated relationship, add one more variable to a previous design, or test hypotheses from someone else's "theory." In general, if such studies are done because of their feasibility and expediency, the results will not have a great deal of impact and you will not experience very much satisfaction from your achievement. Having said this, we also realize that there is a great deal of useful research that is of the nuts-and-bolts variety and that fills the role of replication and generalization. However, a major consideration is whether such research is done because the investigator is interested in and committed to the substantive questions themselves or whether it is simply an expedient way to complete projects and get published. The latter may result in a lack of thorough preparation in the subject matter and a lack of thorough preparation for implementing the study.

(9) Research in most fields tends to be faddish. Ours is no exception. Think twice before jumping into a research area because it is "current." The fad may have run its course by the time your project is finished and your contribution may be minimized. Also, following the fads rather than your own interests may lead to a very superficial kind of preparation that will not serve you well.

SUBSTANTIVE SUGGESTIONS

In the course of conducting the surveys reported in Chapter 2 and Chapter 3 and in talking with participants in the Greensboro workshops, a number of suggestions were made for substantive research questions that deserve attention in the future. Some of them seemed more fully articulated than others. We simply list them in Figure 5.2 for whatever heuristic value they have for the reader.

Reading through the list reiterates a number of themes that we have already talked about. There is a strong emphasis on descriptive research and a strong emphasis on trying to identify the cognitive processes that explain why a rater evaluates another person's performance in a certain way, why people search for jobs in the way they do, or why individuals deal with goal setting in the way they do. There is virtually no emphasis on testing a theory.

Does all this imply a strong trend away from conceptual development and basic research? We do not think so. In our opinion, the sum of all these data suggests instead that our conceptual and theoretical work should be more in the language and the reality of the world of work (Daft & Wiginton, 1979) rather then in the prevailing language of journal articles and questionnaire behavior. For example, "testing" Vroom's (1964) expectancy theory via questionnaire measures of expectancy, valence, instrumentality, and self-rated effort is far different from using the same theory to guide a study of what really facilitates and/or hinders a group of individuals in a particular kind of job. The theory is most useful when it tells us what questions should be translated into the language of the organization and then used to study *behavior* in organizations.

We are not at all sure what it means to "test" such models, whether they pertain to motivation, leadership, job satisfaction, or problem solving. They are not unitary structures that must be true or false. We think the field has a greater need for theory than ever. We need guidance as to what questions are

(text continues p. 146)

FIGURE 5.2   **A Summary List of the Research Problems Most Frequently Mentioned by Survey Respondents, Interview Respondents, and Workshop Participants**

Recruitment

- We know very little about job search behavior (except, perhaps, for new college graduates) and how pools of applicants for jobs are actually formed. There is a lot of theory that can be brought to bear here and a lot of useful knowledge to be gained.

Job Analysis

- We need a series of comparative studies on the *construct validity* of various methods of task description and job analysis. That is, do they exhibit the appropriate kind of reliability, do they sample the job representatively, do they miss infrequent but crucial components, do they produce accurate descriptions as determined by replication, judgment of incumbents, and matching of jobs to descriptions?

- What are the limits of job evaluation methods for determining the equal worth of jobs? Can equal worth be *reconceptualized* to make it more amenable to measurement?

- What are the different problems faced by public administrators that are not faced by managers in private organizations, and vice versa. What are the implications of these differences, if any, for management selection and training?

- We seem to need a series of human engineering studies on the skills and abilities that will be required for a number of different jobs as the age of microelectronics comes upon us. What will the jobs of "secretary," "office supervisor," "purchasing agent," "accountant" be like in terms of their ability requirements?

Performance Measurement

- Using cognitive models from the study of person perception, research on memory, and the study of complex problem solving, we need a series of studies on how raters form judgments of others' performance. "Implicit theories" of performance, H. Simon-type heuristics, recall phenomena, stereotypes, perceptual biases, and attribution of cause are all phenomena of interest in describing the process by which one individual observes the behavior of another individual and forms a judgment about his or her "performance."

- When making performance judgments, what specific *goals* do raters have in their heads? That is, what are they trying to do? How do

FIGURE 5.2 Continued

the goals raters have change as the result of the performance rating situation (e.g., routine appraisal period versus promotion time; "good" employee versus "bad" employee)?

- What are the major problems people see in the way their performance is judged? How would they like their performance to be judged?

Selection

- Can simulation or job sample methods be used to test for problem-solving and decision-making ability? What model should be used for such test development? Is it all a matter of heuristics that are specific to particular problem areas? Can it be distinguished from general intelligence? How can the problem-solving behaviors in a job be sampled? How can good problem solving be distinguished from ineffective problem solving in a job context?

- How can the physical ability requirements of jobs be defined more precisely? How can the physical components of tasks be sampled and assessed at selection?

- We perhaps need a massive series of Monte Carlo studies that would map out the limits of the generalizability versus specificity of validity and that would give an indication of the extent and kinds of information that are necessary in a predictor/criteria domain to infer generalizability.

- When examining the validity of prediction information in a selection situation, have we relied too exclusively on the model of a performance dimension as a single dimension where "hi" and "lo" scores are simply a function, more or less, of the characteristic(s) measured by the predictor (as implied by validity coefficients or expectancy charts)? Suppose we devoted at least some research resources to analyzing the major, but specific, reasons for *failure* (i.e., being a low scorer) and then ask, given a particular "score" on a predictor, what is the probability that a particular kind of failure would be exhibited? This *discrete failure* model would suggest a different kind of predictor selection.

- What is the construct validity of self-evaluations on various dimensions (e.g., abilities, job performance, leadership)? What parameters bias such evaluations?

- How can jobs be redesigned and selection methods altered to better accommodate handicapped individuals?

(continued)

FIGURE 5.2 Continued

EEO Considerations

- What are the effects, if any, of affirmative action programs on those hired because of it and on those already in the organization? What parameters seem to determine positive or negative reactions to such programs?
- What is the actual extent of racial tension in U.S. organizations? What are the major forms that it takes?
- In the validity/fairness/adverse impact domain, the principal models and points of view have been explicated. If we now had a series of sensitivity (i.e., Monte Carlo) analyses that would give some idea of the actual costs (i.e., in terms of productivity gains and losses and minority group gains and losses), we could then begin to press everyone's nose to the wall and determine what value judgments people actually want to make. That is, what is it that various groups of people really want to optimize in all this?

Turnover/Retention

- It might be possible to formulate a *substantive* model of attrition/retention instead of a general "box model." Rather than path analysis perhaps a more appropriate analytic technique for such a task would be a Markov process within which it would be possible to talk about the probability of staying or leaving given the specific situation of an individual. Adopting a Markovian type framework would get away from looking at correlations between general summary indices and would force the investigator to talk about specific states (defined by educational level, age, length of service, wage rate, job satisfaction score) and the probability of staying/leaving given membership in that state. The retention problem has been studied long enough to do this and parts of such a model already exist.
- We need more detailed investigation of turnover as a construct. How much is really under the control of the individual? How much is really under the control of the organization? How much is voluntary, but simply unavoidable? How can people in these various categories be identified? What kinds of turnover can specific interventions reasonably be expected to influence?

FIGURE 5.2 Continued

Training and Development

- As preparation for developing more effective *substantive content* for training in problem solving and decision making, the problem-solving and decision-making behavior of real managers and administrators could be described and analyzed in terms of the elements that seem to characterize bad decision making and those that seem to characterize good decision making. Both the context and the behavior should be analyzed. For example, what are good decision-making heuristics in a *particular domain* of management decision making?

- How can supervisors be trained to deal with employees with special problems (alcoholism, physical handicaps, and so on)?

- How can basic skills (i.e., the 3 Rs) be taught most effectively to adults who need employment but who have educational deficiencies? This is a plea for research on substantive content and learning events (e.g., precisely what is it about arithmetic that should be taught) *not* the learning media (e.g., Is CAI better than a live instructor?). In general, training research has been too media oriented and too little research attention has been paid to the structure and content of what is to be learned.

Leadership

- The following "model" or "theory" of leadership should be researched in terms of how to select and train leaders. To wit: Leadership is composed of the following major "roles" and the trick is to select for, or train for, competence in each of these roles. One advantage of these roles is that a lot is already known about what constitutes competence in at least some of them. They are:
  (a) A leader models appropriate performance.
  (b) A leader understands the task well enough to help subordinates set reasonable, specific, and frequent performance goals.
  (c) A leader is a teacher and trainer (and thus must be competent in something analogous to basic instructional design).
  (d) A leader practices functional behavior analysis and tries to describe subordinate behavior in terms of the contingencies that currently control it.
  (e) A leader is a controller of at least some rewards on a one-to-one basis.

(continued)

FIGURE 5.2 Continued

(f) A leader facilitates the smooth interaction of his or her group.

(g) A leader accurately and fairly judges the performance of each subordinate.

- All trait theories of leadership aside, might there be a measurable construct we could call leadership aptitude? The trait approach foundered originally on using emergent leadership in small groups as a criterion. Might a better criterion lead to something? There *are* people who consistently seem to be better leaders than others, are there? What should be assessed within the framework of this construct? How is it related to subject matter expertise, general intelligence, and so forth? Should leadership aptitude be conceptualized as unifactor, multidimensional, or what?

Motivation

- For various large populations, we need detailed and comprehensive descriptive studies of what people think about their jobs, their job context, their "careers," and so on (no questionnaires please). What do they like? What do they not like? What helps them? What hinders them? What are specific things they would like to see changed? Why do they do certain things? Why do they not do certain things? What specific things do they hope for? And so on. There is a good deal of "theory" that can be used to structure the interview content and it should be used to its fullest advantage.

- Much of motivation theory is directed at explaining variability in "effort." We really do not know what effort is. We have no even minimally valid measures of effort. However, we can measure choice behavior (e.g., the choice to work or not to work on a task). Can a wider variety of choice situations be identified and measured such that they can serve as useful and valid dependent variables for investigating motivational questions?

- Specific goal setting, the public portrayal of task goals, and frequent feedback are powerful determinants of performance, and much more could be done with developing these strategies. It is not enough for managers/officers/administrators to have specific goals in their heads or in their files. New technologies must be developed for facilitating the formulation of specific goals, for portraying them visually, for providing feedback efficiently, and for dealing with dysfunctional side effects that might occur. It is the goal-

---

FIGURE 5.2 Continued

---

formulation, goal-portrayal, goal-accomplishment, feedback, goal-recalibration *system* that is an important topic for study and development.

- Although goal setting is labeled as a cognitive area of investigation, as yet there have been no systematic attempts to find out how people process information about goals. When are goals recognized as goals? Along what parameters do people evaluate goals? And so forth.

- Functional behavior analysis is a powerful strategy for understanding behavior in organizations. Unfortunately, few of us who study organizational behavior are skilled in its use and it is easy to misapply the strategy. In spite of this, it would be useful to begin a controlled expansion of this kind of research into additional aspects of organizations. For example, an examination of major performance problems, communication difficulties, and resistance to policy changes could profitably be examined from this perspective. The importance of the descriptive phase of the strategy cannot be overemphasized. It forces the investigator to be very concrete and explicit in specifying the behaviors to be studied and identifying the contingencies that *currently* control them. The clarity introduced by just this descriptive phase may be worth the effort of using the method.

- In the context of more basic research, investigators should begin manipulating job content to see how it influences the way people perceive or cognitively interpret the nature of their work. Given that it is important to know how people perceive and interpret the nature of their jobs, studies of how these perceptions correlate with other perceptions (usually measured within the covers of the same questionnaires) do not tell us much about the jobs themselves. The organization still does not know what it should do about changing them or leaving them alone.

- "Participation" in decision making is one of the most widely used treatments (for various ailments) in all or organizational psychology and yet we know very little about how it is perceived and "cognitized" by its participants, or *why* it works or does not work. That is, what are the mechanisms by which participation has its effects (e.g., goal setting, creation of more positive rewards, more

---

(continued)

FIGURE 5.2 Continued

---

intense punishment for failure)? There are now some reasonable models to use to investigate the processes involved in participation decision making, and they should be put to use.

- What are the best *long-term* strategies for generating and maintaining effective safety and/or energy conservation behaviors?
- How does inflation affect pay perceptions and pay satisfaction? How does it influence judgments of equitable payment?

Unemployment and Job Stress

- What is the array of principal stressors that work situations place on families (e.g., dual careers, long commutes, long hours, boring work, low pay)? What are their principle consequences for family life? What remedies, if any, seem to help (e.g., flexible time)?
- Given the major types of unemployment, what hinders effective job search? What facilitates job search?
- What is job stress? Is there good stress and bad stress? How many facets are there to this construct? Is the same kind of stress punishing for some people and rewarding for others? In general, more work needs to be done to explicate this construct.

Organization Development and Analysis

- Why is so much decision-making behavior under the control of such immediate payoffs? What are the structural characteristics that are really responsible? What are the forces in the organization that actually drive out planning behavior or longer term contingencies?
- What is the specific nature of the socialization process for new employees in specific occupations? Is there an enormous number of such "scripts" describing what goes on? Just a few? What are their major parameters? What are the major consequences of the socialization process itself?
- Much could be gained from an analysis of how individuals react cognitively to organization development methods. For example, how do employees react to a survey of organizational problems, what happens when a "team building" strategy is implemented, and so on?
- When a new innovation is developed, used, and supported by one group in an organization, how can its continued use be facilitated when its ownership is transferred to a new group?

FIGURE 5.2 Continued

- What are the negative consequences of frequent management rotation (as in the military or "growth" industries)? How can they be avoided?

Organizational Effectiveness

- We need a series of "policy-capturing" studies dealing with what people mean by productivity in various contexts. Certainly there is no "true" definition of productivity but there must be a reasonably small number of major ways that people think about it. If we could just arrive at some reasonble taxonomy of the alternatives it would help the national debate considerably.

- To help explicate the meaning of organizational effectiveness and using a variety of methods, we need a comprehensive study of organizational performance *mistakes,* or things that were done wrong. The result would be a substantive categorization of the important kinds of performance dysfunctions people see, and their best description, or guesses, about the causes. The categorization could be done separately for major functional specialties and organization levels (i.e., first-line supervision). We would then have a fairly systematic description of things that need remedial action by means of management policy changes, new training efforts, additional applied research to explore the problem further, or even basic research on the general issues involved. Further, it should be possible to point to classes of performance problems that seem to be a function of major independent variables such as faults in leadership, skill deficiencies, poor job design, poor communication, and the like.

- It would be useful to study the model of "effectiveness" held by various parties (e.g., top management, middle management, rank and file) within selected organizations. What major kinds are there? How disparate are they? What kinds of conflicts do they point to? What do they imply about productivity? The study would be dangerous because it may expose things better left alone and the powers that be may have the mistaken notion that if disagreement exists it is a sign of weakness in the organization.

Methodology

- In general, with regard to such questions as the effect of job redesign, the effects of job previews, the effects of a new incentive

(continued)

FIGURE 5.2 Continued

system, and so on, a research link that is often missing is a study of the cognitive "process" that goes on within the subject. Admittedly, this is difficult research to do and is often open to competing explanations, but it would be valuable. For example, it would be informative to know how applicants react to a job preview. Do they give it any credibility? Do they understand it? Do they think it made a difference in their reaction to their first job experience? The basic research problem here is to develop methods for how such processes can be studied.

• How can the case study be developed into a useful method for assessing the results of complex interventions? (e.g., How specifically and in what form must the objectives of the intervention be stated? Where are the major sources of error in the method? What techniques promote inter- and intra-interviewer agreement as well as inter- and intra-interviewee agreement?)

really important and guidance as to how data gathered on the questions can be interpreted. Theories that are at least in part based on experience, that take account of the ecology of organizational behavior, and that are intended to function as heuristics seem to be in the shortest supply. These opinions are similar to those voiced by Jenkins (1980) for cognitive psychology, by Mc Guire (1979) for social psychology, and by Lundberg (1976) for the study of organizational behavior.

Having disposed of any number of lesser evils, we now turn to something a bit more controversial. While it does not quite fit with the general structure of this chapter, we feel it is an extremely important influence on the question-generating behavior of researchers. It is too important not to mention.

THE EFFECTS OF THE "PUBLISH-OR-PERISH" CONTINGENCY[1]

In our opinion, one of the most harmful influences on the development of research problems is the "publish-or-perish" contingency that exists in some academic departments. We refer to those departments that promote academic staff on the basis of the *number* of items that they publish, rather than the impact or usefulness of the individual's work.

It seems reasonable to expect that this kind of reinforcement contingency will promote certain kinds of behavior on the part of reasonable people. To be specific, a premium will be placed on studies that are feasible, easy, economical, and short. The usual assistant professor tenure of five to seven years is not very long, and the risk of spending time on research that cannot be publishable quickly in a number of pieces must be minimized. This contingency also promotes so-called piecemeal publication, and publication of the same thing in as many different places as possible. As journal editors, two of the authors frequently had the experience of receiving a paper that was sent to two different journals at the same time but the wrong cover letter was put in the wrong envelope, or sending a paper to a particular referee and finding out that the same paper had also come to the same referee from another journal. On the face of it at least, this kind of contingency should also reinforce the falsification of data. No one knows how many fraudulent data there are in the journals. We hope there are not very many and that the reinforcers for being honest still rule the day. However, it is worrisome and we do not feel comfortable about it.

Given its dysfunctional consequences, why is the "pay for the number of titles" strategy maintained? Most likely because it is perceived as objective, quantifiable, and reliable and because alternative strategies are seen as too difficult to maintain. However, if a nonacademic organization used an appraisal strategy like this, most industrial/organizational psychologist would evaluate it negatively. All kinds of arguments would be offered for why it is dysfunctional. In some respects, the emperor indeed has no clothes and we should admit it and get on with trying to remedy it.

However, the burden of change must not be placed on the back of the individual investigator. We (who already have tenure or for some other reason do not need it) cannot self-righteously admonish individuals not to submit to this contingency when in fact they must live within it. Instead, we should point our attention toward the management of the academic units involved. As with any organization, these units *must* spend time defining what they want their faculty to *do*, and we hope it is not things like "producing three titles in refereed journals per year." If a goal of the organization is to have its faculty do research that makes an impact on the field, then that is what should be judged. It is not five publications of the same thing that have an impact. It is not administering one unvalidated questionnaire to one sample and breaking it up into five published reports that has an impact. It is not looking around for a variable to add to someone else's study or testing a hypothesis from someone else's theory that has an impact. The management of the college or department must evaluate everything the individual has actually done and decide whether the individual is making a large enough contribution to deserve promotion. Frequently, work that has a great impact on the field is not published. Most often, if a major study is presented in one piece it will have much more impact than the same study published in six little bits. It is the substance of the work, not the form, that has an impact. There is a large literature on performance assessment that can guide the managers of the academy. They should use it.

Finally, and most emphatically, we are not trying to argue that academic researchers should not be evaluated against very demanding performance goals. Indeed they should. Much, much more than three titles a year should be demanded. Useful and expert research that indeed makes a contribution is what should be rewarded even if it results in no journal publications for a particular year. We should be rewarding excellence, not the ability to be pedestrian. If the structure of the research enterprise and the contingencies by which it lives prevent this, then we must collectively devote some effort to planning how to change our system.

A FINAL, FINAL WORD

In a treatise like this it is a bit too easy to focus on the negative, rail against the ignorant and the misguided, and create the impression that everyone (except us) needs help. We hope we have not done that. Rather, our intent was to satisfy the instructional objectives we outlined at the outset as best we could.

We also did not want to create the impression that complex answers to complex questions will come easily if only the people in the field will get themselves straightened out. As with most aspects of the behavioral sciences, the study of industrial psychology and organizational behavior is complex business. Both research and practice are very, very difficult to do. Consequently, we do ourselves a disservice if we unthinkingly adopt unrealistic goals and expect near-perfect explanation or prediction of organizational phenomena. A historical case in point is our constant fretting over the criteria problem and the "ceiling" on predictive validity. In some significant way we seemed to buy the notion that there is an ultimate criterion, if only we could find it, and that near-perfect predictor of it is possible. These are very counterproductive expectations that lead to much guilt, self-doubt, and beliefs that the field is not going anywhere. We actually know quite a bit about how the criterion problem and the selection/prediction decision should be modeled and about why the prediction of long-term performance from a brief sample of information obtained from applicants cannot produce near-perfect predictions.

The moral of all this is that we should accept the complexity of the phenomena with which we deal and the conflicting value judgments that are a part of criterion assessment, motivational practices, equal employment considerations, and all the rest. Given the complicated world, we should compare what we do to what is possible and not to some unreachable ideal. To this end we have tried to reflect the state of our question asking and some possible strategies for improving it as fairly and as accurately as we could.

NOTE

1. The views in this section are those of the first author, who feels strongly about them. Professors Daft and Hulin are gentlemen and scholars, but they do not necessarily agree.

Appendix A

February 20, 1981

TO: Participants in the Innovative Research Questions workshop
        (workshop #2) to be held at the Center for Creative Leadership
        (March 25-27) as part of the Division 14 sponsored conference
        on (gasp) innovations in methodology for studying organizational
        behavior.

FROM: John Campbell
        Richard Daft
        Charles Hulin

RE: Some introductory remarks about procedures and expectations

For over a year the three of us have worried, and worried, and worried
some more, about whether there was anything for us to say on this topic.
We are still worrying. It does seem rather presumptuous to anoint oneself
as an expert on what research questions are good or bad, how research
questions can be improved, or how investigators can become more innovative.
The probability of drowning in a sea of self-righteous pontification is a
bit too high.

To protect against such a fate, we have attempted where possible to
gather empirical data and to stay away from overly authoritative pro-
nouncements. We also have tried to focus on the identification of major
research needs, as well as considering how to ask "better" questions.

Objectives

Having said all this, the objectives of this workshop, as they have been
retranslated from the original, are as follows.

1) To describe the research questions that are currently being
   asked in our field and to comment upon some of their more
   interesting characteristics.

2) To report what various people think are the most important
   research needs that we have and to contrast the questions
   that have been studied with the questions that people think
   should be asked.

3) To describe the characteristics that seem to distinguish successful question asking from unsuccessful question asking, as it is
   practiced by some of our more successful researchers.

4) To illustrate and summarize the principal strategies that might
   profitably be used to reformulate research questions.

5) To illustrate and summarize some of the strategies to be
   avoided when formulating research questions.

Procedure

To aid in accomplishing these objective we did the following things.

1) Surveyed the available literature on creativity, research innovation, research shortcomings, historical comments on our field, crystal ball gazes into the future, etc..

2) Content analyzed a sample of the research literature.

3) Surveyed a large sample of opinions about what research needs should have high priority in the future.

4) Interviewed, at some length, a sample of established researchers in our field. The respondents were asked to describe a study they had done that they were proud of and a study that they were not so proud of, and might like to forget. For each of these two situations the origins of the research questions, and the way it was developed were contrasted. We have called this the "within investigator" study.

5) Labeled ourselves as experts.

Instructional Objectives

The workshop will discuss the findings produced by the above activities and their implications. What we hope that you come away with are:

1) Some specific knowledge about what the field is investigating versus what people think it should be investigating.

2) Some specific knowledge about how the more accomplished investigators in our field seem to develop their research questions and what, if anything, distinguishes a successful vs. unsuccessful question-generation process for these people.

3) A list of substantive research ideas, at least some of which you might consider seriously in the future.

4) Familiarity with a number of different strategies that can be used to reformulate research questions, or otherwise look at a problem differently.

5) Knowledge of some major sins that should be avoided when formulating research questions.

6) Enough new resource material to make some significant change in the way you teach, or otherwise try to influence, others to generate and develop research problems.

A Request

Everyone should remember that this particular conference is not meant to be the end of the "innovations in methodology" development process. An important goal is to learn things from the invited participants such that these additional facts, strategies, and ideas can be incorporated in the subsequent development of materials for wider dissemination. Consequently, it would help us if you would do some serious thinking during the next few days and would contribute your thoughts and biases when the opportunity arises. Specifically, try to give some thought to the following.

1) What do you think should be our highest priority research in the near future?

2) What do you think makes a specific research question useful or not useful?

3) What characterized the question-asking phase of a successful research project with which you were involved?

4) Are there "conventional wisdoms" (i.e., about methods, theories, findings, etc.) that hinder our approach to certain problems?

5) Are there implicit but widely shared value judgments in your (our) field that act to constrain or inhibit research?

6) Do you have any favorite methods for stimulating students, colleagues, etc. into thinking about research problems differently or more productively?

See you in Greensboro.

Appendix B

June 25, 1980

TO: A Sample of Division 14 Members

FROM: John P. Campbell

I am writing for a very special reason. In 1981 Division 14 will sponsor a large conference devoted to innovations in research methodology. It's a major effort that the Division has spent two years planning and implementing. One section of the conference will be devoted to issues pertaining to the identification, generation, and evaluation of <u>new research questions</u> in applied psychology in general and industrial/ organizational psychology in particular.

One issue concerns what people both inside and outside the field see as the major <u>research needs</u> that should occupy us during the next 10-15 years. Consequently, we are trying to sample individuals from a number of different populations about their opinions concerning future research needs. One of these populations is the Division 14 membership. Others are the American Academy of Management, "real" managers and administrators, union personnel, and government administrators/legislators. If we could obtain a good sample of each group's opinions, it would then be informative to compare the research questions that are actually being asked with the research questions each of these groups says should be asked. To this end I am contacting approximately 250 members of the Division.

The specific purpose of this memo is to ask you to give us your most articulate, well-reasoned, and thoughtful statement as to what you think are our most important research needs. There is room for a list of six needs on the attached pages; however, any number from one to 50 would be helpful and appreciated. Use additional pages if you want.

A "research need" could pertain to some theoretical question that you think is important; it could focus on some problem area in organizational life that needs research. We are not so worried about getting precisely the right frame of reference as we are about you giving us you best statement about where you think future research should be directed. Do be as specific and as concrete as you can.

In sum, I hope you will give this some thought over the next few days, jot down your ideas, and return the attached pages within the next few days. You can contribute significantly to this cooperative effort to lead ourselves in new directions.

Appendix C

A List of Research Suggestions from Survey Respondents That Were Judged to Be Very Brief or Very General

GENERAL SUBSTANTIVE TOPICS

- Develop more measures with good construct validity.
- Need new research methods.
- Use the information processing model.
- Do process research.
- Study dual careers.
- Standardized definitions, measures, and/or indices of major variables and constructs (e.g., absenteeism, "motivation," unemployed).
- Study underemployment.
- What explains productivity?
- Integrate theory from several fields.
- Integrate macrostudies with microstudies.
- Do research on research implementation.
- Combine clinical and experimental methods.
- Study career motivation versus work motivation.
- Determine relative contribution of selection versus training.

- How should people deal with "conflicting demands?"
- Need better program evaluation.
- Need better individual coping strategies.
- Determine impact of government regulation on productivity.
- Study the effect of government regulations on leader behavior.
- What organizational environment is best for managerial and technical productivity?
- How do successful managers manage?
- Are climate surveys any good?
- Identify rewards for specific groups.
- Need better methods for observing behavior.
- Should study "new" organizational forms.
- Determine what really motivates people.
- Study vigilance behavior.
- Study informal communication.
- Study irrationality.
- Study novel behaviors.
- Integrate the many small theories into a few larger theories.
- Describe circumstances under which people *really* change (e.g., change jobs, file a grievance).
- Do cost/benefit analysis of I/O techniques.
- Study invasion of privacy.
- Use a development model.
- Study role of personal values in organization behavior.
- Study psychological processes.
- Study work versus nonwork.
- Study career development.
- Study individual rewards.
- Study organization politics.
- Study labor market issues.
- Study worker health.
- Develop new sources of selection information.
- Determine interaction of appraisal strategy and individual motivation.
- Study nonlinear phenomena.

- Investigate the parameter of "time" as it pertains to many relationships.
- How should we measure change?
- Study the effects of inflation.
- What "turns off" motivation?
- What is leadership?
- Go beyond 2-factor theory of leadership.
- Reanalyze the full potential of group process research.
- Humanize technology.
- Determine how to improve training.
- Develop unobtrusive measures.
- Study person/environment fit.
- Do research that bridges individual and group levels of analysis.
- Do longitudinal research.
- Determine interaction of selection, training, and job design.
- Study ethical issues.
- Validate organizational behavior research findings.
- Study midcareer malaise.
- How can we reverse the decline in the quality of human beings?
- Determine what theories are the most valuable for translating into practice.
- Study self-management.
- Determine how employees cope with life.

SUGGESTIONS FOR PARTICULAR ORGANIZATIONS OR POPULATIONS TO STUDY

- Small organizations, new organizations, temporary organizations
- Unusual organizations (orchestras, Sierra Club)
- Agribusiness
- Government organizations
- Foreign versus domestic organizations

- Small groups as simulations of systems
- Unions
- Other cultures
- "Service" jobs
- The aging work force
- Old versus young workers
- MBAs

Appendix D

**Interview Protocol and
Questionnaires Used in
the Within-Investigator
Study Reported in
Chapter 4**

American Psychological Association

Division 14

Innovation in Methodology Task Force

Questionnaire for within-person comparison of successful and unsuccessful research projects.

Instructions. Please think back over research projects you have been involved in and identify one that you would consider quite successful and one that was not very successful. The notion of a research project includes all kinds of empirical research as well as theoretical papers intended for academic publication.

Both projects should have been *completed, written up, and submitted for publication.*

The *successful* project would be one that received positive acceptance by reviewers and colleagues, perhaps been cited, generated positive feedback from readers, and recognized as making a contribution to the field.

The *unsuccessful* project would be one that was not accepted in a positive manner by colleagues, received little recognition, perhaps was never published even though submitted to several journals.

Authors' Note: The mean response for each questionnaire item for each type of study is shown in parentheses.

Procedure. Please complete two questionnaires, one for the successful project and one for the unsuccessful project. The initial questions are open-ended. Later questions ask you to rate the project on five-point scales.

I. *Background and Origination of Study*

    A. First, can you explain to me the general idea and purpose of the project?

    B. How did the project originate? For example, where did the idea come from, how was it developed, and so on? (Interviewer — *probe like crazy to obtain the complete picture because we know almost nothing about this part of the process.*)

    C. What was there about the project that excited or attracted you at the time?

    D. Has it been published?   Yes _____
                                   No _____

    E. What is the best single reference for this material?

    F. Was the project successful in the sense that it received positive acceptance and feedback from reviewers, reprint requests, perhaps citations, and was generally accepted by the field?   Yes _____
                               No _____

    G. What things (role, organization context, reward system) do you think facilitated or hindered the origination of the project? (Probe about feelings at the time if not volunteered.)

    H. What do you see as the major contribution of the research project?

    I. If project was unsuccessful, why?

II. Motivation for the study

Now I am going to ask a series of questions about your motivation for doing the project. Please respond on the basis of a five-point scale that represents the extent to which the statement applies to the project. A "1" means the statement applies to a very little extent and a "5" means to a very great extent.

TO WHAT EXTENT WOULD YOU SAY THE PRIMARY REASON FOR YOUR RESEARCH PROJECT . . .

	Little Extent		Ratings	Great Extent		N/A
	Not-So-Significant			Significant		
1. . . . was to apply a new research method or technique as a way to shed light on a well-established research problem	1 (2.2)	2	3	4 (3.3)	5	9
2. . . . was to test previously established relationships on a new sample of organizations or organization participants	1 (2.3)	2	3	4 (2.0)	5	9
3. . . . was to add a new variable or new combination of variables to the study of an established phenomenon	1 (2.7)	2	3	4 (3.2)	5	9
4. . . . was to use an improved, more rigorous method than was previously used to study an established phenomenon (greater internal validity)	1 (2.4)	2	3	4 (3.3)	5	9
5. . . . was to adopt and use a method originally developed for use in another field of research	1 (2.2)	2	3	4 (2.3)	5	9
6. . . . was to bring together ideas from two or more fields or subfields of study	1 (2.7)	2	3	4 (3.0)	5	9
7. . . . was to explore an issue or problem that was frequently discussed and of current interest in the literature (timely)	1 (3.3)	2	3	4 (3.6)	5	9
8. . . . was to investigate a topic because it was controversial or in dispute	1 (2.6)	2	3	4 (3.3)	5	9
9. . . . was to address a problem clearly identified in the literature, perhaps pointed out by other authors as needing investigation	1 (2.3)	2	3	4 (2.7)	5	9
10. . . . was to test directly competing theories or models about a phenomenon	1 (1.8)	2	3	4 (3.0)	5	9
11. . . . reflected your personal interest and curiosity rather than acceptability and interest to the discipline	1 (3.4)	2	3	4 (4.2)	5	9
12. . . . was the opportunity to use a method that was convenient for you to execute (familiarity, expense, facilities, etc.)	1 (3.0)	2	3	4 (2.4)	5	9
13. . . . was the discovery or availability of a data base that enabled you to test ideas that were interesting to you	1 (2.4)	2	3	4 (2.1)	5	9
14. . . . was the potentially important application to organization functioning (world needs it)	1 (2.6)	2	3	4 (3.0)	5	9

III. Outcomes (results) of the Project

The next questions pertain to the outcome or result of the project as reflected in the final written draft for publication. Please respond on the basis of the same five-point scale.

TO WHAT EXTENT DID THE PROJECT . . .

	Little Extent		Ratings	Great Extent		N/A
			Not-So-Significant	Significant		
15. . . . identify a relationship between variables that previously were believed not to be related	1 (2.0)	2	3	4 (3.0)	5	9
16. . . . provide evidence that a previously accepted relationship actually has the opposite sign (now − instead of + or + instead of −)	1 (1.7)	2	3	4 (2.4)	5	9
17. . . . provide evidence that a previously accepted causal relationship is actually in the opposite direction ($x \rightarrow y$, not $y \rightarrow x$)	1 (1.6)	2	3	4 (1.5)	5	9
18. . . . determine that diverse phenomena are united by a single explanation (simplification or integration)	1 (1.7)	2	3	4 (2.9)	5	9
19. . . . provide evidence that a standard phenomenon (construct) is actually composed of several subparts (e.g., diversity)	1 (1.6)	2	3	4 (2.4)	5	9
20. . . . develop a new explanation for an already accepted relationship between variables	1 (1.8)	2	3	4 (2.6)	5	9
21. . . . provide evidence that a phenomenon previously argued to be bad (inefficient, immoral, dysfunctional) is actually good (efficient, moral, functional, or vice versa	1 (1.3)	2	3	4 (1.7)	5	9
22. . . . show no relationship where one was previously believed to exist	1 (1.5)	2	3	4 (2.2)	5	9
23. . . . have implications that apply to the real world, such as being useful to managers or to teachers of introductory O.B. and I/O psychology courses	1 (2.2)	2	3 ·	4 (3.7)	5	9
24. . . . apply to organization settings or individuals in general (rather than to limited type or to limited population within organizations)	1 (2.5)	2	3	4 (3.4)	5	9
25. . . . develop a new theoretical construct or variable for use in the field	1 (2.0)	2	3	4 (2.2)	5	9
26. . . , provide results that were statistically significant	1 (3.0)	2	3	4 (3.7)	5	9
27. . . . help resolve a controversial or disputed issue in the literature	1 (2.0)	2	3	4 (3.4)	5	9
28. . . . clarify a poorly understood or cloudy issue	1 (2.6)	2	3	4 (3.9)	5	9

IV. General Characteristics of the Final Paper

Finally, a few questions about the project in general. Please think in terms of the same five-point scale.

TO WHAT EXTENT . . .

	Little Extent		Ratings	Great Extent		N/A
	Not-So-Significant			Significant		
29. . . . was the general topic area of the paper mature, well established and widely studied (e.g., leadership, satisfaction, administrative ratio)	1 (2.8)	2	3	4 (3.1)	5	9
30.						
a. . . . did you have firm expectations about the empirical outcomes	1 (2.6)	2	3	4 (3.6)	5	9
b. . . . if so, to what extent did empirical results differ from your expectations	1 (1.9)	2	3	4 (2.1)	5	9
31. . . . would you say the methodology and argument were systematic, sound, rigorous, tight and relatively error free . .	1 (2.6)	2	3	4 (4.3)	5	9
32. . . . did the paper criticize previous research as a way to justify the project . .	1 (2.4)	2	3	4 (3.3)	5	9
33. . . . would you say the methodology might be perceived as complex and sophisticated by the intended audience . .	1 (2.8)	2	3	4 (4.0)	5	9
34. . . . did you weigh the potential publishability of the results before undertaking the project	1 (2.6)	2	3	4 (2.9)	5	9
35. . . . was topic considered "hot" at the time	1 (3.0)	2	3	4 (3.0)	5	9
36. . . . was the project exploratory and open-ended so that you were uncertain about the findings (asking a question rather than testing hypotheses)	1 (3.4)	2	3	4 (2.7)	5	9
37. . . . were the variables of interest quantifiable in an objective rather than subjective fashion (e.g., size easily quantifiable as counting # of employees; power is illusive and intangible)	1 (3.1)	2	3	4 (4.0)	5	9
38. . . . was the research a logical stepwise extension of research previously published by yourself or others	1 (2.6)	2	3	4 (3.2)	5	9

References

Barrett, G. V. Symposium: Research models of the future for industrial and organizational psychology. *Personnel Psychology,* 1972, 25, 1-17.

Bass, B. M. The shadow and the substance. *American Psychologist,* 1974, 29, 870-886.

Center for Creative Leadership. *A summary of programs and activities.* Greensboro, N.C., 1982.

Cronbach, L. J. & Gleser, G. S. *Psychological tests and personnel decisions (2nd ed.).* Urbana: University of Illinois Press, 1965.

Daft, R. L., & Wiginton, J. C. Language and organization. *Academy of Management Review,* 1979, 4, 179-191.

Davis, M. S. That's interesting! Toward a phenomenology of sociology and a sociology of phenomenology. *Philosophy of Social Science,* 1971, 309-344.

Delbecq, A. L., Van de Ven, A. H., & Gustafson, D. H. *Graph techniques for program planning.* Chicago: Scott, Foresman, 1975.

Dunnette, M. D. *Fads, fashions, and folerol in psychology.* Paper presented to Division 14 at the American Psychological meetings, Chicago, September, 1965.

Dunnette, M. D. Research needs of the future in industrial and organizational psychology. *Personnel Psychology,* 1972, 25, 31-40.

Dunnette, M. D. *Mishmash, mush, and milestones in organizational psychology: 1974.* Paper presented at the American Psychological meetings, New Orleans, August, 1974.

Ford, R. M. *Motivation through the work itself.* New York: American Management Association, 1969.

Gergen, K. J. Social psychology as history. *Journal of Personality and Social Psychology,* 1973, 26, 309-320.

Gordon, W. J. J. *Synectics: The development of creative capacity.* New York: Harper & Row, 1961.

Gottfredson, S. D. Evaluating psychological research reports: Dimensions, reliability, and correlates of quality judgments. *American Psychologist,* 1978, 33, 920-934.

Jenkins, J. J. Can we have a fruitful cognitive psychology? In *Nebraska Symposium on Motivation.* Lincoln: University of Nebraska Press, 1980.

Kasperson, C. J. Psychology of the scientist: A relationship with information channels. *Psychological Reports,* 1978, 42, 691-694.

Lundberg, C. C. Hypothesis creation organizational behavior research. *Academy of Management Review,* 1976, 2, 5-12.

McGuire, W.J. The yin and yang of progress in social psychology: Seven koans. *Journal of Personality and Social Psychology,* 1973, 26, 446-456.

McGuire, W.J. *Toward social psychology's second century.* Paper presented at the American Psychological Association meetings, New York, August, 1979.

Meadow, A., & Parnes, S.J. Evaluation of training in creative problem solving. *Journal of Applied Psychology,* 1959, 43, 189-194.

Meehl, P.E. Theoretical risks and tabular asterisks: Sir Karl, Sir Ronald, and the slow progress of soft psychology. *Journal of Consulting and Clinical Psychology,* 1978, 46, 806-834.

Meier, N.R.F. Assets and liabilities in group problem solving: The need for an integrative function. *Psychological Review,* 1979, 74, 239-249.

Newell, A. You can't play 20 questions with nature and win. In W.G. Chase (Ed.), *Visual information processing.* New York: Academic Press, 1973.

Osborn, A. *Applied imagination* (3rd ed.). New York: Scribners, 1963.

Prince, G.M. The operational mechanisms of synectics. *Journal of Creative Behavior,* 1968, 2, 1-13.

Prince, G.M. *The practice of creativity: A manual for dynamic group problem solving.* New York: Harper & Row, 1970.

Schaude, R.G. Methods of idea generation. In Gryskiewicz, S.C. (Ed.), *Creativity Week I: 1978 proceedings.* Greensboro: Center for Creative Leadership, 1979.

Science Policy Research Unit, University of Sussex. *Success and failure in industrial innovation.* London: Center for the Study of Industrial Innovation, 1972.

Stein, M.J. *Stimulating creativity* (Vol. 1). New York: Academic Press, 1974.

Stein, M.I. *Stimulating creativity* (Vol. 2). New York: Academic Press, 1975.

Vroom, V. *Work and motivation.* New York: John Wiley, 1964.

Webb, W.B. The choice of the problem. *American Psychologist,* 1961, 16, 223-227.

Zand, D.E., & Sorensen, R.E. Theory of change and the effective use of management science. *Administrative Science Quarterly,* 1975, 20, 532-545.

About the Authors

JOHN P. CAMPBELL is Professor of Psychology and Industrial. Relations at the University of Minnesota. His principal research interests are in decision making and problem solving, training and development, leadership, performance assessment, and multivariate prediction models.

RICHARD L. DAFT is Associate Professor of Management at Texas A&M University. His research interests have to do with organizational innovation and change, the use of information by managers, control system design, and the philosophy of organizational research.

CHARLES L. HULIN is Professor of Psychology at the University of Illinois, Urbana. His research interests are applications of modern measurement theory to problems in industrial/organizational psychology, the study of interactions between individual differences and organizational characteristics on attitudes and behaviors of employees, and general methodological issues in organizational research.